Beyond The Illusion:
Choices for
Children of Alcoholism

Susan Adlin Balis

HCI

Health Communications, Inc.
Deerfield Beach, Florida

Susan Adlin Balis
Philadelphia, Pennsylvania

Library of Congress Cataloging-in-Publication Data

Balis, Susan Adlin
    Beyond the illusion: children of alcoholism / Susan Adlin Balis.
        p.   cm.
    Bibliography: p.
    ISBN 1-55874-007-4
    1. Adult children of alcoholics   I. Title.
    HV5132.B35   1989   88-30584
    616.86'1-dc19   CIP

ISBN 1-55874-007-4

Publisher: Health Communications, Inc.
            3201 S.W. 15th Street
            Deerfield Beach, Florida 33442

"The future is but a result of
conditions past and present.
Everything is connected,
everything has its place."

Elie Wiesel,
One Generation After

Dedication

To My Children
Jennifer And Randy

Table Of Contents

Preface

Life is never as it appears to be in alcoholic families. Illusion prevails. People are not always who they say they are or even who they think they are. When mother is drunk, the family says she "is not herself." When dad is hung over, they make excuses saying he "has a headache" or "a virus." Because mother declares, "Nice girls don't get angry," little Nancy never feels angry, but often thinks that others around her are angry. When little Joey is feeling frightened or lonely or needy, he will look mature, competent and in control. He does such a good job of looking good that even he might not realize how he feels underneath the mask of competence. These are illusions, both internal and external. They are illusions that distort lives, that begin as ways to survive the ravages of alcoholism on family life and that eventually come to alienate people from the ones they love and even from themselves. This is paradox.

Adults who come from a childhood of alcoholism display a strength in the face of adversity that is truly admirable. They show an exceptional ability to cope with the chaotic life caused by addiction, remain calm in the face of crisis, and assume more than their share of responsibility and burden. Despite these impressive strengths, these very same people will often be unable to change personal behavior that is self-destructive, compulsive or supports the addictive behaviors of someone close to them. This, too, is paradox.

As a therapist I listened carefully over time to the stories of children of alcoholism. I became increasingly aware of the paradoxes, the excruciating dilemmas, the impossible choices, and the internal and external illusions that shape their lives. I came to understand that enveloping themselves in illusion helped children survive the early years. I also realized that maintaining the illusion as adults prevented them from moving beyond the coping strategies of those early years and kept them trapped in a past that they wanted to escape. The writing of this book arose from my conviction that sharing the results of my experiences as a therapist would help both children of alcoholism and their therapists to understand the illusion. For to do so allows one to work with the inevitable disappointments and fears that so frequently lead to incomplete recoveries. Understanding the threats to recovery — the problems that arise as change is initiated — may prevent the premature termination of treatment or the abandonment of hope.

In my work with the families of alcoholism and other chemical dependencies I have been repeatedly struck by the pervasive power of addiction. It wrenches families from their foundations. It destroys the stability of family life. It shatters the sense of well-being and self-esteem. As I look back on my earliest experiences in this work, it was the adults who were also children of alcoholics who were the most striking to me regarding the complexity and the poignancy of their dilemmas. In addition, they were often the ones who found it most difficult to change.

The literature that began to emerge in the early 1980s describing common characteristics and dynamics of adults who grew up with an alcoholic parent was enlightening for people who felt themselves understood, sometimes for the first time. They found in the literature their own experiences described and validated. This new experience had significant therapeutic benefit as it reassured, validated and informed. The new awareness also led to an improved functioning and an increased sense of well-being for some. Using this new information helped people to change.

I found, however, as I treated people over time many of these changes were short-lived. Determination and enthusiasm ebbed as life's burdens continued to take their toll and people were forced repeatedly to confront old situations. The tendency to use old solutions reasserted itself. Intellectual understanding did not result in new behaviors as people faced the high stakes involved in making significant life changes. While the excitement of discovery was initially extremely helpful and provided impetus to experiment with change, the scars from the wounds of childhood had not healed and continued to leave their mark on current functioning. The loss of certain gains or the lack of continued improvement was often experienced as personal failure. When not addressed, this perceived failure further eroded self-esteem that was already worn

thin. Again the paradox as the very work being done to help people
repair the damage sustained in childhood instead further eroded
self-confidence.

I believe that people need a clinician's perspective regarding the
influence of early experiences in an alcoholic family on development, on the formation of personality and on the molding of
behavior patterns. I think it essential that people hear a therapist's
elaboration about how one effects not only behavior change but
also personality change. In order to make informed decisions one
must know what kinds of help lead to what kinds of changes. For
those who want to make the kinds of changes that require therapy,
it is important to understand how therapy works. In addition, I
believe that clinicians need to better appreciate the power of the
experiences of a childhood of alcoholism and to hear the implications both intrapsychic and interpersonal from a clinician working
in both mental health and addiction. Unless these missing parts are
uncovered the illusion remains.

I have chosen language that is free of jargon and a format that
makes great use of personal histories so that the reader will not be
held back by incomprehensible vocabulary and so that profession-
als will feel the immediacy and the power of the children's
dilemmas. We were all brought up in imperfect families with
some suffering more consequences than others. Children brought
up in alcoholic families suffered not just difficult experiences, but
an accompanying denial that led to the development of illusions
that kept them isolated and alienated even from themselves.
Understanding the illusions will hopefully help people to begin a
journey that will bring them out of their isolation and toward the
discovery of themselves.

Acknowledgments

There have been many people, family, friends and colleagues, too many to list separately here, who have helped sustain me over the years it took to write this book. Whether through their interest and feedback regarding my work, their sound advice on the practical aspects of this endeavor or their comfort during the trying times, they eased the isolation that preparing this book required. I thank them all for being there.

Many of my colleagues at the Institute of Pennsylvania Hospital, particulary those of the Social Work Department and the Strecker Program for the Treatment of Alcoholism, were particularly sustaining during this challenging but sometimes difficult endeavor.

There were certain people who worked directly with the manuscript and its publication. I would like to give them special thanks:

Albert Adlin, M.D., Deirdre Laveran, M.S.S., Helen Parke, M.S., and Kathiern Reardon, R.N., all gave generously of their time to read the manuscript and offer invaluable feedback.

Lewis Merklin, Jr., M.D., provided skillful editing and impetus to proceed as I began to think about publication.

Constance Brooks ensured that even the smallest but often most important details would be handled efficiently and effectively.

Jean Rast, R.N., generously shared her knowledge of the publishing procedure while offering reassurance during the more difficult parts of the process.

Sally Russo, M.S.W., provided substantive editorial commentary that helped bring the book to its final form. She also offered encouragement when my own belief in this undertaking faltered.

David R. Burns, M.D., through his incisive critique, helped me discern where to define, explain and elaborate when this was not evident to me. Our ongoing dialogues regarding the treatment of children of alcoholism have been thought-provoking and enriching. This book would not be what it is if not for his gentle provocation and encouragement.

Donald J. Gill, M.D., more than anyone, helped this book take shape. He pointed the way toward organization when there was little more than chaos. His thoughtful criticism enabled me to reach further and deeper than at times I thought I could. Most importantly, he never imposed his own ideas or style but used his creativity to help me cultivate my own.

And finally, I am deeply indebted to the children of alcoholism, both young and old, who have shared with me their stories, their pain and their courage. By allowing me to enter their lives, they have enabled me to write this book.

Prologue:
Setting The Scene

Lives lived under the influence of alcoholism are lives lived under the influence of denial, distortion and deception. Truth is relentlessly compromised — sometimes unconsciously, often unwittingly but nevertheless compromised. Children are victims of those distortions and their lives are shaped in significant ways by them. At the same time, children learn to use denial, distortion and other defenses that deceive in order to survive and to protect themselves in a hostile and uncaring world. Ironically, the very adaptations that children use to survive the devastating impact of parental alcoholism will shape their lives in adulthood in ways that recreate the childhood they so want to put behind them.

I write this book to address the distortions of a life lived in the shadows of parental alcoholism and to narrow the gulf of misunderstanding that separates those who grew up in that shadow from themselves and from the people they care about. Because of the isolation and silence that surrounds such a childhood, the children do not get a balanced perspective on their experiences. Because of their reticence about this aspect of their lives, the people around them are unable to understand or offer them helpful input. It is a tragic lack of understanding. It leaves everyone feeling helpless and inadequate. It does not automatically correct itself just because a child grows up.

As people become more informed about the nature of their problems they are in a better position to do something about them. Understanding what the choices are is crucial because choices and solutions are often unclear to children of alcoholism. Alcoholic and co-dependent parents (the so-called sober parents who are nonetheless caught up in the alcoholic's addiction) present a distorted perspective of reality — I call this illusion — illusion that leaves children feeling confused and unsure of themselves. My intention is to reveal the denial, the distortions, the illusions that surround a childhood of alcoholism, and then examine in depth the maladaptive influences and consequences that childhood has had on their lives. I will then explore how adult children of alcoholics can move beyond that childhood, repair the damage done and enjoy a reality that is not dependent on denial, distortion and illusion to sustain itself. As understanding increases, so does the awareness that one has choices. Options for change and the way change of this nature occurs will be described so that, once again, people understand in a clear and objective way what their choices are.

Denial

Alcoholism and its effects on the family go unrecognized as a result of denial. Denial is a defense mechanism, an unconscious avoidance of thoughts or feelings that would produce conflict if experienced. Thus, the alcoholic, through the unconscious process of denial, is unaware of the alcoholism. This may be hard to appreciate because to an observer the alcoholism is obvious. The alcoholic may realize that he is drinking too much, but rationalizes that he can stop any time — he's just not ready to stop yet. Or the alcoholic may realize that others are concerned with his drinking and then criticize them so as not to take their displeasure seriously. Or he may consistently not recognize that he is drinking too much or that the drinking is problematic. These are defense mechanisms in operation, various ways of thinking about the drinking that prevent the alcoholic from facing the serious problem his drinking has become.

Very often the co-dependent spouse also uses denial. Even if the spouse becomes conscious of the alcoholism he or she may still deny that it is affecting the children. This leaves the children living with a phenomenon that is never acknowledged or explained to them. Living with the denial of an illness that has such profound effects on the quality of life of the family may do more to shape the child's character than even the overt consequences of the alcoholism. Although children of alcoholics are compared to children growing up in other kinds of dysfunctional families, it is the response to the denial that may account for their unique cluster of characteristics.

Defense As Survival Technique

Another phenomenon that separates children of alcoholism from children of other dysfunctional families is the sense that survival, literal survival, is frequently an issue. Alcoholism brings with it accidents, terminal illnesses and violence; all are threats to the life of the alcoholic and the family. Even when children are not the direct recipients of physical abuse, illness or accident, they may see their parents at risk. This is experienced as a threat to their own survival, for if a parent's life is threatened, the child's survival is also in question.

To survive children develop their own defenses. These defenses, which are successful in that they help a child survive a traumatic childhood are not so successful when used to live healthy lives. Using those childhood survival techniques in adulthood often recreates the old scenes. It explains why some people become alcoholic despite avowed determination not to become like their parents. It explains why some choose alcoholics or other substance abusers as partners, again despite their determination not to. It explains why they may develop other disorders or unconsciously seek out mates who are workaholics, gamblers or compulsive in other ways. It explains why, even though they seem to escape untouched, their children may become chemically dependent, despite and maybe even because of their determined efforts to prevent it.

These phenomena will be examined through the stories told by people who experienced a childhood affected by parental alcoholism. It is particularly important to stay with the actual experiences because for most children of alcoholism these experiences have either been denied or so distorted that they have little meaning. By examining the stories and their implications without the distortions of the past, new insights and understanding can arise that help people look at the past, and ultimately the present and the future in a different way.

Mark's Story

When I think of a story to best introduce this material, the one that immediately comes to mind describes a scene which serves as a powerful metaphor for the land in which a child of alcoholism lives. The story-teller is Mark, a forty-eight-year-old highly respected director of a child care agency. At the time he told this story, Mark was a patient in a chemical dependency program in a private psychiatric hospital. With a long history of various physical ailments, Mark suffered from chronic pain and had become dependent on pain medications. Unable to manage his pain without the use of addictive drugs, he had been unsuccessfully through both pain management and substance abuse programs. In a psychiatric hospital setting he hoped to be able to have his medications reevaluated and at the same time find other ways of alleviating his pain. The program's treatment team hoped to help him recognize the psychological sources of his pain, which might then help him to relieve, tolerate or manage the pain more effectively and without the use of drugs.

Mark exhibits many characteristics common to adult children of alcoholics. He entered a helping profession and rose to a position of influence within his chosen field. His wife was extremely loyal to him but the relationship was under much stress because of the demands Mark's illnesses have imposed on it. While both profess great love for each other, they also both point to high degrees of unresolved conflict, unverbalized dissatisfaction and disappointment with each other. Mark had also developed a chemical dependency but insisted to himself that it was in no way similar to his father's alcoholism. He also denied it had any effect on his children. Although Mark's characteristics are typical, they are also extreme. It might be easier to relate to someone with fewer or less severe problems, but Mark's story and Mark's experiences make it easier to see the various phenomena at work because they are so striking. Mark often operated on the parameters, but parameters define the shape of objects and Mark's story highlights and defines, often metaphorically, the childhood of alcoholism.

As part of his treatment, Mark entered a therapy group for adult children of alcoholics. This was his first exposure to information about this subject. Also for the first time, he heard stories of other group members' experiences growing up with an alcoholic parent. It had a powerful impact on him. He had vivid memories of the almost daily physical violence and psychological abuse his alcoholic father had showered on the family, but he had never heard others talking about such strikingly similar incidents. He listened in amazement, clearly moved. But his own first participation in the group had nothing to do with such stories, but instead with the description of how he ran away from home. And the emphasis, the lavishing of detail, was reserved for the scene he described.

It may be that to go directly to the experiences with his father would have caused Mark too much emotional pain and so instead he told a story about running away from home. His use of a physical setting provides powerful images and insight, showing how such a scene may symbolize a life. In subsequent groups Mark recalled incidents when his father tyrannized the family as a result of his unadmitted and untreated alcoholism, but this first time he talked about running away and the land he had to traverse to do so. Mark's story will be used frequently in subsequent pages to illustrate many of the psychological mechanisms utilized by children of alcoholics. For now, however, it sets the scene; it describes the environment so familiar to many children of this land.

Usually quiet and reserved, Mark spoke with great fluency and eloquence as he related his tale. At age fifteen he ran away from home because he stated, "I couldn't stand the life there anymore." It was a cold and rainy day. He ran across muddy fields, getting soaked by the rain and chilled by the relentless wind. He did not know where he was running; he just knew he had to keep going. Suddenly he found himself in the path of an oncoming train. He was terrified. He rolled down an embankment and landed in an icy river to avoid the train. Drenched, shivering and shaking from the near encounter with death, he continued to run, unwilling to return home.

His face softens as he remembers the next part of the story. An elderly couple befriended him. "I stopped at a farmhouse to ask for work. I was wet, muddy, dirty," he shakes his head in wonderment as he continues. "They took me in. The way I looked! I guess they must have seen how young I was. They gave me clean clothes, a hot meal and a comfortable bed. They told me I could work for them. I was so nervous about being late for work the next morning that I tried to stay awake all night. But I must have fallen asleep near day-break. When I woke up the sun was already high in the sky. I was devastated to think I'd be late for work my first day. I found out later that I'd slept for two whole days! Can you imagine that? They let me sleep for two whole days! Out of the goodness of their hearts. I couldn't get over that."

Even as he recounted this story some thirty years later, Mark's amazement seemed as fresh as it must have been that sunny afternoon. He still marveled at the kindness this couple had showed him. He continued to bask in their warmth. His pleasure from the memory had not been dulled by the passage of time. Mark only stayed with this couple for a brief time. A sense of obligation pulled at him and he soon returned home.

Perception

We can look at Mark's story as a reflection of how he perceives his life. In his description, Mark paints two very different pictures. They are of two extremes, one that takes on the character of a nightmare (the childhood of alcoholism) and the other of a pleasant, almost magical dream (the wished-for, idealized childhood). The rain, wind and cold describe a reality that is harsh and bleak and desolate. The oncoming train is life-threatening physical danger and the only escape is into an icy river which is both painful and again dangerous. This serves as a metaphor for incidents that Mark later described where he was in fact physically threatened as his father kicked and punched him in alcoholic rages. Survival seems ever the issue and even survival brings with it tremendous distress.

There are no people in this landscape. Comfort, safety and protection are not there for this young boy. This, too, may reflect the reality because Mark's mother, who loved him and cared for him when she could, also could never fully protect him (or herself) from his father's abuse. It seems that Mark already had learned not to turn to others when survival was the issue. Mark's survival depended solely on himself; he did not look for help or rescue when his life was at risk. It is important to remember this later, in the exploration of how children of alcoholism can repair the psychological damages once they are revealed. The need will be always to do it alone, never to look to others for help. While in the situation Mark described, his survival depended on focusing sharply and single-mindedly on his own resources. That tendency will not help him to treat his addiction, to resolve his difficulties with his wife and to improve his functioning at a time when an improved relationship, not physical survival, is the issue.

There is a radical shift to the next part of Mark's story where he describes a land that is just the opposite. It is warm and sunny and provides safety, protectiveness and nurturing for young Mark. In this setting he is not alone. There is a friendly couple to take care of him, to feed him, to let him sleep when he needs the sleep and to not expect too much of him. This may represent Mark's dream for a better life: to be unconditionally cared for and nurtured. This is a dream he has never been able to realize. The desire for total satisfaction and contentment may only be attainable through the use of drugs, and specifically, drugs to kill pain.

Mark deals in extremes in his story, a common tendency when one comes from the kind of childhood Mark describes, but a tendency that brings with it serious problems. The idealization of the farm couple is a common fantasy of children of alcoholism — that other families lead perfect, storybook lives. This makes their own lives seem even more desolate by comparison. In addition, by idealizing someone else and someone else's family, Mark appears even less worthwhile in his own eyes. This is one of many ways he finds to confirm his poor self-image.

Both parts of Mark's story have an air of unreality about them. They have more the flavor of tale, dream or nightmare, than they do of memory. This, too, reflects the very nature of a childhood of alcoholism, which is a reality so shaped and mishapen by denial that it becomes surrounded by doubts regarding the authenticity of the events that occurred.

Mark did not say why he returned home after such a short time, but this deserves speculation. Children of alcoholism often return either to the old scene or to scenes that closely resemble those of the childhood despite their avowed determination that this will not happen. Mark must examine the motivations for his behavior because not until those motivations are understood, will he be able to bring his behavior more into line with what he desires for himself. Several possibilities come to mind regarding his returning home so soon. It could have been fear for his mother and the assumption that he had to take care of her. It could have been his own need to return and try to save his father. It could have been a yearning to return to the known, though unpleasant, because at least there was comfort in the familiar. These are the kinds of possibilities that Mark will have to think about if he wishes to understand and then change the repetitive nature of his behavior.

Beyond Survival

Mark was admitted to a therapy group for adult children of alcoholics as a way to begin to unravel the mysteries of his past. Adulthood does not necessarily bring with it the automatic clarification of a past that has been shrouded in distortion and deception. As long as that past remains misunderstood it controls the present in dysfunctional and maladaptive ways. Mark responds instinctively in the present the way he did in the past. Untreated, he will continue to see life through the lens of the past. If this lens distorts and deceives, it will affect his vision of the present. It also will color the way he views and formulates his future.

Through information and the sharing of similar experiences Mark can begin to unravel the past. Groups can provide entry into a more honest reality than one has previously experienced. Therapy is a way to rework the old solutions so that they do not keep recreating an unhealthy past. Mark, an intelligent and sensitive adult, looks back on his past through the eyes of the child who lived that past. He is unable, alone, to remove the distortions, the false assumptions and the unrealistic dreams and wishes of the young boy who endured such trauma. His pain, now physical, follows him into his adulthood, pursuing him relentlessly. He is unable to gain control over it. He must begin by understanding it.

I have written this book to elaborate the details of the experience so that one can ultimately understand it in all of its fullness and complexity. As a clinician who has listened to hundreds of stories of both children and adults who grew up with an alcoholic parent, I am struck by the intricacy of the dilemmas they have faced. I believe it is of crucial importance *not* to simplify and *not* to deny the paradox, the double binds, the unresolvable dilemmas children have found themselves forced to resolve. I have been impressed, repeatedly, with the strength of these children, with their resourcefulness and tenacity in the face of adversity. I have also been impressed with the pervasiveness of the defenses they have used to survive and the tenacity with which they hold onto those defenses when they are no longer needed. The strength and resourcefulness and tenacity must be turned around once again, so that they work for and not against survival, this time a different kind of survival, a survival that has moved beyond mere existence and is now concerned with the quality of life. This book is written to that end.

The Childhood

The Illusion

Part I

There is a discrepancy between the actual experiences of the children and the way these are interpreted to the children by the parents. This discrepancy I call illusion. Events are filtered through the distortions of the alcoholism. These distortions are the result of the extensive use of certain defense mechanisms that sustain the addiction, defenses such as denial, minimization, rationalization and avoidance. Particularly, denial plays a major role in shaping the events of family life. Denial, as described earlier, is an unconscious process that protects people from the conflict they would experience if they became aware of the thoughts or feelings being denied. The drinking behavior is minimized or denied, but so, too, are the responses of the other family members to the drinking. Thus, what the children see and feel and what the parents *say* about what the children see and feel differ and are even contradictory. This presents the children with painful dilemmas as they struggle with such questions as: "Are my parents lying to me?" "Am I really seeing what I think I'm seeing?" "Can I trust my own perceptions?" "Am I crazy?"

Irreconcilable Contradictions

Life is replete with paradox and contradiction. When these are neither acknowledged nor reconcilable, particularly difficult problems are presented to the children. The parents' denial of the alcoholism does not allow them to acknowledge, and even leads them to deny the unpleasant events surrounding the drinking (e.g. hangovers, late-night drunken fighting). When children overhear or witness such scenes that are then not acknowledged, this is experienced as a repudiation of what they have seen or heard. This may be the beginning of the self-doubt that becomes a profound part of the character structure of many adult children of alcoholics. This leads to asking those troubling questions: "Are my parents lying to me?" "Am I really seeing what I think I'm seeing?" "Can I trust my own perceptions?" "Am I crazy?"

When the event is not acknowledged, then the feelings that are a response to the event cannot be acknowledged either. The emotions that surround such events are often powerful: fear and terror, anger and rage, sadness and despair. But how can one express reaction to an event when the event is denied? Thus children are left feeling utterly alone with powerful thoughts and feelings for which they can find no outlet and no constructive means of expression.

To attempt to answer the question "Are my parents lying to me?" puts children in a terrible bind. To answer yes defames the parents' character and brings into question the idealized omniscience of the parent. But to say no challenges the child's ability to perceive accurately and leads to the even more frightening question: "Am I crazy?" Therefore, children are faced with an irreconcilable dilemma, and nowhere to go for help to resolve it.

Children are left to find their own solutions. Without a parent to model the negotiation of contradiction and complexity, children may not adequately develop beyond their early grasp of the world as seen in very simple, black and white terms. The recognition of the wide range of "grays," involving the need for compromise, the integration of differences and an acceptance of the infinite complexity (and therefore richness) of people and situations, may be lost or at least grossly underdeveloped.

One solution is a massive confusion and an inability to trust one's perceptions. Reality itself becomes a permanent puzzle and the child cannot trust even his own senses to unlock that puzzle. Eli lived with just that kind of reality.

Eli's Story

For Eli, contradiction and confusion always seemed to revolve around his father. In the community Eli's father was a highly respected high school teacher, loved by his students and an active, sober church member, who was admired by the mainly blue-collar congregation. Eli saw the way his father was regarded in the community and it confused him. At home the picture was very different. The image of his father shifted from warm and respected to cold and indifferent, frequently ominous and, at times, frightening. Eli suspected that these shifts had something to do with alcohol and how it affected his father but this part of the image is hazy and unclear. "I never actually saw him drink, but I knew he did. His personality changed. And I could smell it. But I'never actually saw him drink," mused Eli.

Now in his early fifties, with hair graying at the temples, Eli had the quizzical expression of a little boy as he recalled those early years. It was the puzzlement of a young, inquisitive child whose reality (the reality of seeing, smelling and feeling) never was verified by his parents. It was a reality shrouded in mystery and secrets, form never constant, solid or reliable.

"I think he beat up my mother. I never saw that either. But he would say to her, 'I'll get you later.' Now, what else could that mean?" he asks rhetorically, bitterly. He shook his head, silent with his thoughts. And then there were the times when the reality was clear. But even this reality could be denied, distorted or manipulated so that once again it posed irreconcilable dilemmas for Eli.

Eli frowned as he recalled a scene when he was six years old. His sister was eight. He loved his sister. She often protected him from his father's violence. He paused, as if reluctant to continue. "My father pushed my sister down a flight of stairs. We had to take her to the hospital. She was badly hurt. She had a concussion, several broken bones and other internal injuries." He shook his head again, this time with a look of disgust on his face. And then he added, "My mother was there, too. She didn't say a word! But she knew. And I knew, too," he blurted out, hurt and confusion thickening his voice. Eli fell silent, unable to say more. Truth had been twisted, perverted and a whole family made the victim. Unknown to Eli he, too, had fallen victim, victim of denial, of lies, of cover-ups, of a reality compromised and distorted in the service of his father's alcoholism and his mother's misguided attempts to cope with it.

The deception Eli witnessed might have been easier for him to live with had it been consistent with the messages he received from his parents. It was not. His father was regarded as a paragon of virtue in the community. He was seen by others as honest, kind and humanitarian and also saw himself that way. When his behavior was not congruent with his value system, which happened when he drank, he denied it, not only to his family but also to himself. Thus Eli experienced what looked like a moralistic posturing. At the same time he may have sensed his father's sincerity, unaware of the denial that kept the contradictions between his belief system and his behavior deeply hidden from himself.

To compound the confusion for Eli, his mother, who did not drink and who appeared truly sober, played out the *same* seemingly hypocritical contradictions. She doted on her children, protected and even overprotected them at times: but when it came to protecting them from the consequences of their father's alcoholism, suddenly her protectiveness vanished. She scolded the children for their little white lies and then practiced major deceptions as she covered up her husband's drinking and cruelty from the world and denied them to her children.

She did not confront her husband's violence or his lying. She did not protect her children from their father. That would have seemed to be cruel or indifferent behavior. Yet Eli sensed her concern and her love. Why did it fall so short? Why did it not protect them? Eli glossed over his mother's contradictory behavior as if he could not bear to touch or see it and only let himself feel the confusion.

Confusion

The confusion Eli manifested, and which is so frequently described by adult children of alcoholics, has more than one source. Even though he is an adult when describing these events, Eli seemed to be reexperiencing the actual confusion of the child who is developmentally unable to comprehend paradox and is therefore left with an irreconcilable and inexplicable reality.

Confusion also serves as defense. It is a way to avoid feeling the powerful, unacceptable feelings he experiences as he contemplates those old but still painful memories. He quickly moves away from his mother's behavior because that might threaten to be even more contradictory and more irreconcilable than his father's.

The confusion and the accompanying self-doubt are frequently described phenomena of children of alcoholism. They lead to significant difficulties around problem-solving, expressing opinions and maintaining one's position in the face of disagreement with others. Constant self-doubt erodes self-esteem. The automatic retreat into confusion prevents a true understanding of one's feelings and, as a consequence, does not allow for an expression of feeling around conflictual situations where such expression would be a productive response.

By the time adulthood is reached, confusion and self-doubt not only have become *consequences* of the irreconcilable contradictions faced in childhood, but they also have become the automatic *response* to conflict-ridden situations. These responses, arising as they do from early experiences, will not disappear just because one wants them to. Much exploring, in-depth understanding and becoming conscious of previously unconscious reactions will be necessary before the confusion and self-doubt can properly abate.

Inconsistency

Carl's Story

Inconsistency adds to the confusion and further distorts the picture. Carl started treatment for his alcoholism at age thirty-four still not realizing that his binge-drinking father was also alcoholic. An alcoholism counselor began exploring Carl's past with him, including an examination of his father's drinking. Only then did Carl begin to make sense of experiences that previously had made no sense at all.

Carl's father was a binge drinker who would seem normal for weeks, sometimes months at a time. Life at those times would also seem normal. Then his father would start to drink. Gone was any semblance of normalcy. At those times, day to day existence was fraught with inconsistency. "The rules were always changing," he remembered, "and I never knew why. One day I had a pocketful of money; two days later my father would not give me lunch money. At times I had no curfew. I could be out half the night and he would not complain. And then, out of the blue, I would suddenly have to be in at nine o'clock. It didn't make any sense."

Not only did it not make any sense, it also did not provide Carl with a solid knowledge base from which to operate. There was no inner sense of security that clearly articulated, consistently enforced rules and setting of limits might promote. Nor was the environment predictable enough to allow the opportunity to plan ahead and to have reasonable expectations about the future based on past experience. It was as if Carl floated in a world not anchored to a past and present. This world could not inform, direct or ground him in a solid, stable and predictable reality.

Not only were the rules of the household inconsistent, but the lifestyle as well. "My father was a housing contractor but our house was always a mess. The living room sat half painted for years. Nothing ever worked. And there were no rugs on the floor." "But," he exlaimed, "we had a yacht at the shore!" He shook his head with a bitter smile on his face and exclaimed, "No rugs at home and a yacht at the shore!" And on that yacht, he went on to explain, there were *never* any curfews and the money always flowed bountifully. The yacht was always in perfect condition. The sofa at home had cigarette burns all over it, but the yacht sparkled and shone.

Carl never connected his father's erratic, inconsistent behavior with alcoholism. His father always worked, was never physically violent or obviously drunk. No one in the family talked about his father's drinking and certainly no one ever described it as alcoholism. Carl simply lived with the inconsistencies, attaching no meaning to them and having no context into which to put them. Like Eli, this left Carl confused and at a loss in a world that made no sense.

Denial

Denial is a frequently used psychological defense mechanism of the alcoholic. When used as a psychological defense, denial is an *unconscious* process that enables a person to disavow unacceptable thoughts, feelings or even events. This type of denial enables the alcoholic to continue to drink despite disastrous consequences. Denial is also used *consciously* in the alcoholic family to avoid dealing with the unpleasant repercussions of the alcoholism. In both cases, denial can shape children's perceptions of reality and affect the way they experience the world.

To the child of an alcoholic family, denial becomes a way of life. For not only is denial symptomatic of the alcoholism, it also rapidly spreads throughout the entire family system. The sober parent often denies the alcoholism as much and for almost as long as the alcoholic, making excuses for the drinking behavior and minimizing it. There may be several reasons for this. Misunderstanding and misinformation about the disease of alcoholism may lead people to misdiagnose it. If one believes that alcoholism is a sign of moral or character weakness instead of an illness, it will be impossible to identify one's respected and respectable spouse as alcoholic. "He only drinks on weekends," "She never drinks in the morning," or "He's never missed a day of work," are all frequently used (and incorrect) reasons why the alcoholic is not identified as alcoholic by the family.

Misconceptions based on a spouse's early contacts with alcoholism — whether it was a parent or the neighborhood drunk or the black sheep often whispered about in the family — will lead a spouse to believe that alcoholism is a hopeless, intractable condition. The spouse will therefore be unwilling or unable to admit that the alcoholism exists.

Even if the sober parents recognize the alcoholism, they may still try to hide it from the children. Denying it to the children becomes a misguided attempt to protect them from its impact. The most devastating impact on the children is the parents' denial that alcoholism is affecting the children. This denial spares both parents the pain of acknowledging how their children are suffering as a result of the family's troubles.

Denial, Past And Present

Lois illustrates the experience of the denial both as child and later as adult. I interviewed Lois while her husband Larry was in an inpatient setting for the treatment of his drug and alcohol abuse. Larry, a thin, sarcastic, bitter young man, is the opposite of his wife who is heavyset, pleasant, solid and respectable looking.

While discussing Lois's life, I asked her about alcoholism in her family of origin. She quickly and emphatically said that there was none. However each time she talked about alcohol she would grimace or roll her eyes. I asked her to describe her parents' drinking. She said her mother did not drink at all but that her father drank every weekend. "He was not an alcoholic," she insisted, "because he drank only on weekends." When asked to describe his drinking she winced and said, "Well, I never knew what to expect when he drank. Sometimes, but not always, mind you, he'd pass out on the kitchen floor. I could never bring friends home since I could never be sure if I'd find him passed out on the floor."

This conversation with Lois exemplifies two frequently described phenomena that result from the denial in the alcoholic household. The disease is never diagnosed ("He only drank on weekends") but still it controls her life. Not bringing friends to the house is commonly used as a solution for children trying to hide the embarrassment of a parent's drinking behavior from their friends. It isolates them and entrenches a sense of shame resulting from undefined parental behavior that is often experienced as a consequence of their own inferiority.

Lois continued. "Sometimes, but not always," she reassured me, "he'd rant and rave until two or three in the morning. Sometimes I'd even hear crashing objects. But when I looked for them in the morning, I never found anything."

What she did find in the morning was denial. A denial so palpable it must have felt like she was crashing into a stone wall. As she bounded into the kitchen her mother quickly and sternly told her to be quiet; her father had a headache (not a hangover) and was sleeping. Lois must not disturb him. She then went on to prepare breakfast as if nothing had happened.

One cannot help but wonder what it was like for Lois as she raced into that kitchen. What fears was she experiencing and what comfort and reassurance must she have wanted from her mother to quell those fears? She could not express fear or ask for comfort if the event is not acknowledged. Did she then wonder about her ability to perceive accurately? Did she ask those questions I first posed: "Did I really hear what I thought I heard? My mother isn't acting like there was a big fight last night. Can I trust my own perceptions? Am I crazy?"

The dark side of the denial is that it never gave Lois validation that her perceptions were accurate and her emotional responses were appropriate and worth expressing. But there also may be a comforting side to the denial. It must have been a great relief for Lois to rush into that kitchen and find her mother there, safe and uninjured, quietly preparing breakfast. Denial allowed them both to focus not on the horrors of the night before but on the safety of the present, on the fact that they survived the darkness of the night and could be together in the well-lit kitchen of the morning.

When I ask Lois how her father's drinking affected her mother, her response reflects this position. "Oh, she was fine," she replied blandly, "she went to work every day." The focus is on the survival, and if denial helps keep that focus steady, then denial will be used increasingly by Lois as she attempts to survive her childhood.

Lois reflected denial as she talked to me. She had no memories of any strong reaction to those episodes and she showed no curiosity at all about the old scenes. Lois never heard her mother question her father's behavior or confront it. She never heard the word alcoholism used. From her parents' behavior she learned *not* to ask questions and *not* to think about certain behaviors but just accept them. This lack of curiosity is still with her.

This was evident in the way she approached her husband. Her husband had warned me that she knew only about his alcoholism but not about his drug abuse. It turned out that she certainly *did* know about his drug addiction but there were very significant gaps in her knowledge. She just had never let him know what she knew. And she had no curiosity about what she did not know. He would stay out all night and she never questioned this or what it meant.

This may be the same use of denial she experienced with her mother. To protect herself from what she did not want to know and from what she might be *afraid* to know, she suddenly lost her curiosity and became insensitive to her husband's behavior. Her lack of curiosity is a self-protective avoidance of a reality she dares not face. When there is a chance that the answer to a question will be too painful, Lois does not ask.

Although it is easy to see the self-protective nature of Lois's lack of curiosity, it is important not to lose sight of the fact that this is not normal. Lack of curiosity is a true loss for Lois, albeit an unrecognized one. Children are naturally curious. It is how they learn and explore their world. Not being curious restricts and confines them, limits them, ages them. Adults who can maintain that curiosity about life are possessed of a precious quality because it prevents them from becoming jaded and worn. It also enables them to continue to grow, question and learn.

Although children possess a natural curiosity, they do not always know how to ask questions that will give them the appropriate answers. Attentive parents can help a child learn to focus or form their questions in ways that will satisfy their desire to know. Carl tried to question things that puzzled or troubled him but he got no satisfactory answers. He also seemed to run into the same concrete wall that Lois encountered. Lois's response was to put blinders on herself and go through life only seeing half of what was presented to her. For Carl, the response is a pervasive confusion.

Denial Confounds Perception

Carl remembers the first time he saw his father passed out on the living room sofa. He looked dead. Carl was terrified. He shook him, cried, yelled at him to wake up, but his father did not move. He ran for his mother. She looked angry. She muttered that his father was just asleep and that Carl should not bother her. She did not tell Carl that her anger was not meant for him but for his father and the drinking. She was too upset by the scene with her husband the night before (he had not come home until 3 A.M. and then passed out on the sofa) to take notice now of how upset her son was. Nor did she think to comfort him or reassure him or tell him what was happening. With no outlet for her own fears and anxiety the night before, she had been unable to fall asleep. In the morning, tired and worried, she went grimly on with her cleaning, tense and in silence, barely noticing her son.

Still trembling from the shock he had just experienced, Carl retreated. He felt confused. He peeked in at his father again, this time from a distance. His mother said that his father was only sleeping. Why then did he look different than he usually did when he slept? Was this difference he sensed all in his mind? Was he just imagining things? His mother often accused him of that when he started asking a lot of questions about his father. Could he trust his own perceptions? There was no one to ask. Nor could he realize, locked as he was into the isolation that so frequently encircles the alcoholic family, that there were other children from alcoholic families asking the very same questions.

Perception for Carl becomes compromised at this point. He cannot trust his senses. What he heard from his mother and what he saw for himself contradicted each other. His mother told Carl that his father was just sleeping, but when Carl looked at his father he felt a sense of dread. Could he trust that sense? The scene might appear normal but then again it did not. Again those questions: "Is my mother lying to me?" "Am I really seeing what I think I'm seeing?" "Can I trust my own perceptions?" "Am I crazy?" A repetitive pattern of denial such as this has so confused and unnerved Carl that he continues to reflect it thirty years later.

He is often reluctant to make known his perceptions or opinions for fear he will be contradicted. To be contradicted is always a devastating experience for Carl because it calls into question his ability to perceive or think accurately. As a result, he frequently retreats into confusion rather than acknowledge perceptions or feelings. And when the feelings become uncomfortably strong, rather than acknowledge them, he questions his own sanity. Almost in a whisper, his eyes reflecting a fear he cannot express, he haltingly mumbles, "Sometimes I feel like I'm crazy."

Denial To Protect An Image

Ruth, a young nursery school teacher, illustrates another kind of denial. She was well aware of her father's alcoholic drinking, his unending criticism of her and her siblings as well as his very obvious cruelty and physical abuse. It was hard for her to find pleasant memories in her childhood because they were so colored by her father's alcoholism. But she did have one. She smiled and a dreamy look came over her face as she said, "My mother baked wonderful homemade bread. I loved her bread." When I asked her to elaborate on this she hesitated and then her smile became fixed and her eyes looked hard and angry "My mother went to any lengths to keep the peace," she continued hesitantly. "At the table, she always served my father first. He took all the meat. We kids got the leftovers. The vegetables and bread." She paused, the smile relaxing again, "I loved her homemade bread."

I was not sure I had heard her correctly and so I asked, "Your father took *all* the meat?" Her smile again rigid and her eyes glassy, she responded, "Yes." "Couldn't your mother have reserved some for you, perhaps in the kitchen?" A look of amazement now spread over her face. "I never even thought of that," she remarked. "All I remember is how much I loved her homemade bread." Ruth had staunchly focused on her father's cruelty so that it enabled her to deny to herself major deficits in her mother's ability to take care of her.

Again we see how self-protective is denial. Ruth, unprotected by *both* parents, protected herself by maintaining an image of her mother as protective. Her idealization of her mother's bread seems to represent a distortion of reality, an insistence that her mother adequately nourished her and protected her from her father's greed. At the same time she denied her own needs (for a proper, well-balanced meal in this instance) *and* the failure of her mother to properly meet her needs.

Denial becomes a way to survive denial. When children spare themselves from having to answer the unanswerable questions posed by the parents' denial and when they spare themselves the terrible pain of facing the realities of alcoholic living by screening out much of it from their awareness, they have denied certain realities to survive them. Although this may be a relatively healthy response to an unhealthy situation, it will not serve well in healthier times. The ongoing, prolonged use of denial in difficult situations will eventually lead to more problems or prevent people from seeing problems that could then be resolved. Although denial starts out as a survival technique, it eventually jeopardizes the quality of life. It must be remembered that denial is an unconscious defense against anxiety and its use will not be recognized by the user. Because of this, adult children of alcoholics must look to others for help as they work to reduce the amount of denial they use in their lives. This, too, will pose dilemmas for them because they have learned not to trust what others tell them. This will be explored further in the chapter on therapy, but should be noted now as the roots of this dilemma arise from the situations described here.

The Price Of Confrontation

Jackie has a vivid memory of her first overt encounter with her alcoholic father's denial. A name or explanation had never been given for her father's erratic, sometimes violent behavior. One day someone came to her school to describe to the children the symptoms of alcoholism and the benefits of AA in treating it. She was amazed to discover her father's behavior being described and put into an understandable context. She filled with excitement. Now that she had an explanation for his behavior she felt that all she had to do was explain it to her father and the nightmare she had been living through would finally come to an end. She grabbed up all the AA literature that was offered. She rushed home from school, barely able to contain her enthusiasm. Carefully she prepared an explanation for her father based on what she had learned that day. Armed with brochures and bubbling with hope, she began to tell her father about his alcoholism.

At first he laughed, dismissing everything she said as inapplicable to him. When she persisted, he flew into a rage. He bellowed that she was an ungrateful, disrespectful liar who had no right to talk to him that way. He then tore up the literature she offered him, beat her and locked her in her room. Jackie had expected her father to react with gratitude and relief when she uncovered the truth. Instead, she encountered his rage, violence and an absolute denial of the realities she was experiencing.

Intrusion Of Adult Reality

In families of alcoholism reality becomes compromised, distorted and denied because of the response to the alcoholism. So much is hidden from the child that reality is experienced as erratic, confusing and without plausible meaning. However, there are times when children are exposed to adult realities that they should be spared.

Marjorie remembers the last time she had a friend sleep at her house. They had stayed up late to play (her mother was out drinking) and fell asleep on the living room floor. They were awakened by sounds coming from the sofa. It was her mother and a strange man whom she had brought home with her. Word about the incident traveled like lightning throughout the neighborhood and Marjorie's friends were no longer allowed to sleep at her house. Marjorie struggled with her inarticulateness to tell this story, barely able to put the words together to describe the event.

Another young man, struggling with similar issues, went to the other extreme, as if reality was so repugnant to him that he dramatized it in order to reduce it, to distance from it and to make the listener question its veracity. (Marjorie stammered and whispered as she spoke, perhaps for the same reasons.) The young man told his story in a mock childlike voice, frequently pausing for dramatic effect:

> "I remember the Christmas I found out there was no Santa Claus. Both my parents had started drinking early Christmas morning. They promised me Santa Claus was coming. I always connected Santa Claus with my parents. I waited. My mother's best friend was there too. I kept asking when Santa Claus would arrive. They kept drinking and promising me he would come. The day dragged on. I went to my room to wait. I waited all morning and all afternoon. My parents and my mother's best friend continued to drink. Finally, as night fell, I came out of my room. Mommy was passed out on her bed. I went into the living room. Daddy was there. On the floor. He was doing something funny to Mommy's best friend. There was no Santa Claus that year."

For this child the parents' alcoholism, which affected his life in profound and innumerable ways, was elusive, denied. But the illusion of Santa Claus, harmless, symbolic even of the naivete and blind trust of the young child, was shattered by the intrusion of an all-too-adult reality. The play on what is real and what is not, on the innocence of young hopes and dreams and on the sudden intrusion of the forbidden, the taboo, the *un*childlike, still haunt this man. These specters were reflected in his choice of words and the tone of his voice as he told his tale of shattered innocence.

Family Life:

Compromised Structures

At the very beginning of their lives when they are most helpless, it is best for children to feel that they are at the center of a safe, all-protective and all-providing universe. This establishes a basic comfort with themselves and with the world. Gradually, as they develop, they learn that they are not at the center of the world but that there are ways to negotiate with this world in order to get their needs met. Parents who are invested, attentive and nurturing provide the best experience for children learning to gain mastery over their lives. As they increasingly explore their environment and their own rapidly developing capacities, children begin to experience an awareness of their limitations. The inevitable ensuing frustration, when properly modulated, becomes impetus to growth, adaptation and continued development of new problem-solving skills. When parents do not help the children learn to tolerate frustration, it can become overpowering for them. The children's own unaided attempts to master their world will be less successful because they do not have the benefit of an adult's mature input.

The role of the family is to provide a nurturing, safe environment in which children feel secure and free to grow and learn. In this environment children learn to trust and love, develop solid identities and finally separate from the family. In families where alcoholism exerts its influence, the extent to which this occurs optimally is at issue. How much the alcoholism disrupts the family's rituals, controls the family's structures and impinges on the family's ability to nurture, protect and educate its young, will determine how detrimental the effects are on the children. Family organization, generational and interpersonal boundaries, alliances and loyalties all are compromised and distorted by alcoholism. Whether these phenomena are the cause or response to the addiction, the effects on the children are similar.

Organization Around Chronic Crisis

As an addiction takes more and more hold on a family, it begins to control the family, determining how the family functions and is organized. Life in families of alcoholism is often characterized by a state of chronic crisis: medical, economic and social problems are never adequately dealt with and, therefore, repeatedly recur with an immediacy that presents as ongoing, unrelenting crisis.

Medical Crises

Medical crises may arise as a direct result of the toxic effects of the alcohol or drugs consumed. Overdoses, intentional or accidental, occur. Accidents and injuries result from violent or careless behavior. The co-dependents (spouse and children) may also be more vulnerable to medical problems for several reasons. They are sometimes the recipients of violent behavior. As they live chronically with unresolved tensions and pressures, their bodies may react somatically to the stress. Their eating and sleeping habits may be adversely affected. There is a tendency to neglect routine medical and dental care for all members of the family because most of the energy and attention is spent meeting the recurring crises.

Danny's Story

Now a young doctor on an emergency room service in a general hospital, Danny has been making medical decisions since he was a little boy. Both of his parents were alcoholic, though in those early years his father was the more overt one. His mother appeared to be merely her husband's drinking partner. They lived in an affluent, conservative suburb of a large city. Each night Danny's parents would have cocktails before dinner. Danny and his two younger brothers never knew just how long this cocktail "hour" would last; sometimes it was brief and followed by dinner and a relatively peaceful evening. At those times Danny and his brothers could do their homework uninterrupted and get an adequate night's sleep.

At other times, and Danny never quite knew why, this cocktail "hour" might last for two or three hours. On such nights dinner might be forgotten or burned and the children would have to make themselves peanut butter and jelly sandwiches. One night his mother fell down a flight of stairs and neither parent was sober enough to decide if she needed medical care. The decision was left to Danny. On another night his father put a fist through a glass door and again Danny had to treat the cuts. Sometimes his parents would just argue; but on other nights their fighting would become physical and injuries might result. Again, it was usually Danny who decided whether the police or an ambulance should be called. Life in Danny's home was unpredictable and revolved around the consequences of his parents' drinking.

Economic Crises

Financial problems resulting directly from the alcoholism may add to the stresses the family is already experiencing. Often, so much money is spent on the alcohol that it leaves the family unable to meet all of its expenses, creating debts that only become worse as time goes on and the substance abuse remains untouched. Jobs may be lost as a result of the drinking. One young man reported moving eight times in the first seven years of his life because his alcoholic father kept losing jobs. The family could not pay the rent and had to move with every job loss. Each time the child started to settle into a new play group or school he was pulled out again.

Social Crises

Social life may also take on the tensions and unpredictability of living on the edge of crisis. In the early and middle stages of the disease, embarrassing scenes may be more the norm than the exception. A husband gets drunk at parties and starts a fight with a friend, or he makes a pass at a friend's wife. A wife is escorted home by the police when they stop her for driving while drunk. The neighbors are watching behind curtained windows. Police cars arrive late at night, summoned by frightened children to break up the violence of one or both parents. Again there are those silent, unseen witnesses. As a result, the family may become increasingly ashamed and embarrassed and withdraw from friends and relatives.

Neighbors may keep their own children away from the alcoholic's children or treat them with pity and condescension.

Isolation

The growing sense of shame and failure that the co-dependents experience may keep them from confiding in family and friends and thus getting needed feedback, comfort, advice and an outlet for the mounting feelings as the alcoholism gets worse and controls more and more of family life. The family becomes increasingly isolated and insulated which intensifies rather than lessens the difficulties. The isolation becomes a serious problem in itself. Ashamed to admit that something is wrong, the various family members close off options for getting help for the alcoholism. Covering up so that no one will witness the shame the family feels means that there can be no one to call for help when there is a crisis.

And as the alcoholism gets worse there is *always* a crisis. Being alone in a crisis increases the sense of isolation that becomes ever more pervasive. People, both adults and children, begin to lie to cover up not only the problem but also their own sense of inadequacy and helplessness about the problem. As the distance between themselves and others grows greater, the sense that they are different, even inferior, also increases. That sense of being different and being worse than others may entrench itself if uninterrupted. It can become a life-long problem for children growing up in such an environment.

Organization Around The Alcoholism

The organization of a family is related to its mission, which will change over the natural life cycle of the family. In the early years of a marriage that mission will involve the couple organizing their lives together, deciding who will take responsibility for what, establishing relations with the extended family and beginning to create their own family rituals. Once a child is born, the mission will then include as a primary function the nurture and upbringing of the children. The family system will shift to reflect this new mission. As the children grow and need less care from the parents, the organization shifts again to reflect the changing needs of its members. By the time children reach late adolescence parents are preparing to help the children leave the family and start new families of their own. The way a family organizes itself makes a nonverbal but indisputable statement about its values and priorities. This has significant implications for the development of the children and the way the children see themselves.

Family organization is seen through its daily activities, rituals and special times in the life of the family. As a family struggles with an addiction, the addiction and the family's response to it (not the needs of the individual family members) determine how the family will live its life. This is a major assault on the integrity of family life. It also represents major deficiencies in the upbringing of the children of these families.

Mealtime

How mealtimes are structured will reveal much about the life of the family. The mood, the interactions among people and the events surrounding meals will speak to how a given family is taking care of its members. Over and over again, as adults with an alcoholic parent start to talk about and remember their past, mealtime is a source of painful memories and stress. Clearly, for Danny and his brother whether a hot nourishing dinner would be eaten with the family at the dining room table or whether it would be a cold sandwich, hastily and surreptitiously put together in the kitchen so as to stay out of sight of the arguing parents, was determined by how much his parents drank that night. Food, that most basic of human needs, was not guaranteed or assured to Danny and his siblings. To be sure, Danny never went hungry (although some children of alcoholics report going hungry when a parent was too drunk to prepare a meal). But, Danny was only fed on the nights his parents drank too much because Danny himself was able to fix the food. He could not rely on his parents to attend to that most basic need if they had been drinking heavily. What a message to a child!

For Danny and others with this background, there was no reliability or predictability around mealtime. It did not depend on how the family chose to use and structure its time together as a family, but rather on the amount of alcohol consumed by the parents on any given evening. There is a powerful if unintentional message given to children by this behavior. Children deduce from this that they are not important and that their needs are not important either. This sets the stage for life-long feelings of inadequacy and for a preoccupation with satisfying the needs of others to the neglect of one's ability to care for oneself.

Eli, mentioned earlier as the son of an alcoholic teacher who was revered in the neighborhood but feared at home, reports that his family usually ate together. For him, there *was* predictability around mealtime, but it had to do with the inner tension he always experienced at the table. "A couple of times, my father turned over the table, food, dishes and all. So mealtime always made me nervous. I never knew what he might do. I'd find any excuse I could to get away from the table as fast as possible." Mealtime for Eli then became not a pleasant or at least consistent ritual where everyone could be expected to come together at the beginning or end of the day, but rather a time of anxiety when he might be exposed to his father's irrational and violent behavior.

Jeremy remembers mealtime too. His father also turned over the table when angry. Jeremy never knew what his father might do. Sometimes meals were relatively peaceful and family members could relax at the table. Then, suddenly, his father might not like how Jeremy asked a question or reached for a platter and would stab Jeremy on the hand with his fork. For Jeremy mealtime was connected to random sadistic behavior.

Ruth also associates mealtime with her father's alcoholism. "My father had a long and powerful arm," said Ruth. "If you said something he didn't like, he'd knock you off your chair." To keep the peace, her mother made sure that he was always served first. Mother and children wound up eating the remnants of the vegetables and the mother's homemade bread. Ruth, in telling this story, emphasized how much she loved her mother's bread and never questioned why her mother did not provide better for her children. Bread, the staff of life, the symbol of sustenance, became instead a symbol of deprivation and neglect.

The Holidays

Ways of celebrating holidays become an important part of a family's structure. Many adults recalling the early years have bitter memories of holiday times. "My parents always had a fight on Christmas Eve," remarked Marie. "That gave my father an excuse to go out on a drunken binge that sometimes lasted for days. But that was better than his coming home. Because when he came home he usually tore down the Christmas tree." Jeremy remembers his father hurling the Christmas tree across the length of the living room. There was no violence in Becky's home. She insists that her mother's alcoholism "wasn't that bad." But she cannot remember a holiday meal that her mother had ready on time. "Dinner was always anywhere from one to four hours late," she reports, choking back tears of anger. She remembers all those tense and painful holiday afternoons as she watched her mother sneaking drinks, quietly getting drunker and drunker and making up lies as she went along to try to hide the truth from her family. "But it wasn't that bad," she shrugs, as the lines around her mouth tense and her eyes brighten with tears of unacknowledged rage.

Alicia's Story

Alicia describes a Christmas when she was twelve years old. Her father was clearly and obviously alcoholic. Her mother drank along with him but Alicia is unsure whether she was drinking alcoholically also. It made little difference to Alicia and her younger brother and sister because life in their family always revolved around drinking. Her parents went out "partying" on Christmas Eve. Christmas morning they had still not returned. The message that Christmas is a time for children pervades in our society. But at home Alicia received a very different message. The cold, empty house told Alicia that a night on the town was more important to her parents than providing their children with the warmth and joy they saw advertised everywhere. A night on the town became more important than this most important day in the life of a child.

Alicia, showing a perseverance that would provide strength and solace to her increasingly over the years, was determined that she and her siblings have a Christmas. It was a blustery snowy day. Nevertheless, Alicia bundled her brother and sister in their warmest clothes, and they all trudged on foot through the snow three miles to a friend's house so they could celebrate the holiday with a family. Not only had the celebration of Christmas been sorely contaminated for Alicia, but so had the memory of the holiday. This may be a less apparent loss but it is no less significant. With only a bitter memory of holidays ruined, Alicia was then deprived of that special pleasure of expectations of the next Christmas. The joy of anticipation is replaced by the dread, the anxiety and even the depression that often plagues her and others like her as they contemplate holidays and other special events in their lives. Holidays are connected to losses — the loss of pleasurable events and pleasant memories and the loss of anticipation of coming pleasures.

Rites Of Passage

Becky has a memory that illustrates another contaminated structure in the alcoholic family. Rites of passage and the memories of them may also be tainted by a parent's intoxication. As Becky describes her first date in early adolescence, she does not mention how old she was or what she wore. She does not mention the boy or how she felt about him, where they went, how she looked forward to the event, how nervous and excited she was or what happened during the date. What she remembers is that her mother had been drinking all evening and that she went to the door to greet Becky's date drunk.

Not only the event, but the memory of it is spoiled by the actions of another. Many people have disappointing memories of special events in their lives. When the unpleasantness repeatedly comes from the actions of another (one extrinsic to the event) but whose behavior colors the event, then the feeling of being helpless and victimized in a hostile and insensitive world may become powerful and even pervasive.

Megan, now middle-aged and the mother of two teenaged girls, remembered the anticipation of her senior prom. Despite her graying hair and the lines around eyes and mouth, her tremulous voice and facial expression took on the air of an insecure adolescent as she recalled the events of long ago. Like Carl's house, Megan's was always in a state of disrepair, not as a result of financial distress but of the chaos in a house dominated by her father's drinking. She had been dating a boy for months and was "crazy about him." She had managed to have him pick her up at an older sister's house for dates so that he would not have to see the deplorable condition of her house or, even worse, have the humiliating experience of meeting her father when he was intoxicated. Her parents already were beginning to question all the time she was spending with her sister and she knew she could never manage to keep the preparations for a prom from them. Rather than risk the humiliation of letting the boy pick her up at her house, she found an excuse to break off the relationship several weeks before the prom. She not only gave up her senior prom, but also a very special relationship, rather than face the embarrassment of exposing her home life.

This potential for shame and embarrassment is particularly difficult for adolescents, who normally struggle with these issues at this stage in their development. As they come face to face with their emerging sexuality and their growing independence from their parents, the approval of peers takes on a special importance. The fragile sense of self, buffeted by the emerging, sometimes confusing sexuality and issues around dependency and indepen-

dence leaves adolescents feeling insecure and unsure of themselves even in the best of times and in the most nurturing of
environments. As they struggle with the consolidation of their
identities all adolescents are going to have mixed feelings about
their parents and often feel embarrassed by them. To have to deal
with an inebriated parent in front of a date is an experience that is
inherently embarrassing for anyone. Being called on to face this in
adolescence, as Megan and Becky were, even further complicates
the feelings about the parents. It is important to note the strength
here as well as the assault. Each girl still managed to get through
these terrible times, Becky by avoiding her feelings and Megan by
avoiding the event itself. They paid a price for their survival, but
they also manifested a strength that served them well.

For boys, learning to drive is a major rite of passage. It is an event
to be eagerly anticipated, a sign of approaching manhood and a
symbol of growing independence. For Carlos, learning to drive
instead became a part of his father's alcoholism. His father's favorite
bar was several miles from their home. Aware that he was incapable
of driving after several hours of drinking, Carlos's father used Carlos
to solve his dilemma. When Carlos was eleven years old his father
taught him to drive so that he could drive home when his father
had had too much to drink. For Carlos driving was not a symbol
that he had reached a certain level of maturity because he had not.
He was afraid of driving, afraid of having an accident and afraid of
being caught by the police. He was also afraid of the beating he
would get from his father if he refused to drive.

For Carlos, driving was not a source of pride nor a sign of
manhood; it was instead an act to be fearfully and reluctantly
performed in the service of his father's alcoholism. Not only was
Carlos robbed of that special pleasure, a symbolic early step into
manhood, but he also lost a part of his childhood at the same time.
He was pushed prematurely into adolescence, forced to perform
beyond his years and thrust into a pseudomaturity that left him
feeling forever inadequate and ill-equipped to handle life's tasks.

It must have been clear to Carlos that his father was using him,
was less concerned about Carlos and his well-being than about his
own desire to drink. The message to Carlos, whether his father
intended it or not, was that Carlos's needs were not that important
and therefore Carlos himself must not have been that important.
Rites of passage should be affirmations of growth and positive
reinforcement by the family of a child's self-esteem. Instead the

forced pseudomaturity and the inattention to Carlos's needs reinforce the belief in his own inferiority.

Milestones

Rites of passage and other special events such as graduations, birthdays, sports or academic awards, parts in the school play, articles in the school newspaper, playing on a school or Little League team, election to a school or club office, should be times in the life of the family that are focused exclusively on the child. In families of alcoholism these milestones are often influenced by a parent's drunkenness. Parents may not attend special events because they are drunk or hungover. If they do appear and they are drunk, it is even worse because then the child worries about potential humiliation if the parent acts up. Children are also deprived of the parents' genuine pride and undivided attention at these special times because the parents are distracted by their own problems. What should be celebrations are instead times of embarrassment, anxiety and anger at parents not in control of their own lives and unable to attend to the achievements of their children. Rather than boosting the child's pride and morale, these accomplishments are surrounded by negative feelings that contaminate pleasure and assault the self-esteem.

The needs of the children should help formulate and dictate the family rituals; for example, the simple event of the child's bedtime hour should be accounted for in the scheduling of dinner and after-dinner activities. When this is not done, two things happen. First, the children's needs are not properly attended to and this impinges on their healthy development, sense of security and even their health. Second, the children receive messages that their needs are not important and may not be consistently met. This creates anxiety that they will not be protected and safe, as well as feelings that they are not adequate, are not worth attending to, are either unwanted and in the way or are there to attend to the needs of the parents.

Boundary And Role Confusion

Parentified Children

Alicia has other painful memories besides the bleak and snowy Christmas Day when she marched herself and her siblings to her friend's house. She remembers giving her sister a birthday party because she knew her parents would not. She remembers going to speak to the school principal when her brother was in trouble, again, because her parents did not. This behavior points to another compromised structure in the alcoholic family — the confusion of generational boundaries. Healthy families clearly delineate the boundaries between generations and between parents and children. In such families there are clear, well-defined differences between what parents do and what children do. The alliances between the parents are different than the alliances the parents make with the children or the ones children have with each other. Parents do not expect children to perform as parents. Parents do not expect children to side with one or the other parent when parents disagree. Parents maintain privacy about adult matters and do not include children in adult activities or decision making. Although parents may assign tasks and duties to children and may ask children for help in specific areas where children are capable of helping, parents do not expect children to take care of them or act as parents to the parents or to other siblings. The contrary happens in some alcoholic families.

Alicia became a "parentified child." In other words, Alicia assumed parenting functions when her parents abdicated that role. Her mother further confused the generational boundaries when she asked Alicia repeatedly, "What should I do about your father?" This forced Alicia to collude with her mother in an alliance against her father. It also put Alicia in the role of parent to her own mother as she was expected to give her mother advice and look at her father as a troublesome child. Others speak of this role reversal. Janie's mother used to send her to the neighborhood bar to get her father because, "He listens to you. You're his favorite." And Emmy's mother would beg Emmy to try to dissuade her father from going out drinking and then implore her to follow him if she failed to deter him. The implications of this behavior on the part of the nonalcoholic parent is that the child is responsible for the alcoholic's behavior and is expected to control the uncontrollable (the parent's alcoholism). This is a message these children learn well.

In each of these situations roles reverse and children are expected to parent their own parents. It was the same for Danny who had to make adult decisions on whether a scene had become so violent it warranted a call to the police station for help, or whether a parent's injuries were severe enough to necessitate a trip to the local emergency ward. Eli also remembers how his older sister tried to take care of him, diverting his father with chatter of fabricated problems so that Eli could flee from his father's wrath.

Kate's father made it clear that he expected Kate to protect her younger siblings when her mother tried to strike them in an alcoholic rage. When Kate complained to her father he would respond by saying, "Come on now, Kate, be strong. I count on you. I need you to help me with this." Kate reports feeling helpless as she faced her father's demands to perform above her capabilities. She also links this to continued, life-long problems with understanding her own limitations. When her father insisted she perform despite her reluctance, she began to feel that her reluctance, rather than being a sound reaction to an outrageous request, was a sign of her own inadequacy. She continues to assume that demands on her are always justified and is unable to recognize when it is equally justifiable to say no.

Jeremy remembers being five years old and watching in horror as his father tried to smother his mother with a pillow. He tried to get between them to break it up and finally threw water at his father. His fear impelled him to protect his mother. Eventually, he saw it as his duty to protect his mother from his father's violence. Like Kate, the issue of feasibility never entered his mind. It became his mission to do the impossible. His mother further compounded the problem after each crisis when she would complain to him about his father and then ask Jeremy if he thought she should divorce him, fully expecting an answer. How can a child be expected to respond to such a question?

Pseudomaturity

The consequence for children is the development of what is called pseudomaturity. Children learn to find answers and solutions that are really beyond their level of maturity. These children are not as mature as they appear, nor are their solutions always as sound as they appear. They mature with great gaps in their ability to manage life's tasks — to organize, conceptualize and carry through. They may also show great deficiencies in their ability to protect and take care of themselves. Even though they look good and seem to cope at levels way beyond their years, the pseudomaturity masks significant unlearned skills that will provide life-long impediments to smooth, age-appropriate functioning. Internally, also, the price they pay for this superficial maturity is dear, for they live with an ongoing sense of inadequacy, insecurity and failure.

These problems sometimes persist into the third generation. In one therapy group that I led for teenage children of alcoholics, two girls (one thirteen and the other seventeen) described an almost identical experience. What struck me even more than the nature of this experience was the fact that the same thing had happened to two girls in the same small group. The most unusual aspect was that both experiences involved grandparents.

Both girls had an alcoholic grandparent as well as an alcoholic parent. Also, both girls' parents were divorced. The thirteen-year-old Nancy presented her problem to the group. Her mother was getting remarried. Her mother's parents had not spoken to Nancy in two years because that was when Nancy went to live with her father. Nancy's grandparents could not forgive her this "disloyalty" to her mother. Although her mother did not seem particularly upset by Nancy's decision, she also did nothing to ease the tensions with the grandparents. The grandparents, with much flourish, showered gifts and special attention on Nancy's brother, who had stayed with their mother. In contrast, they "punished" Nancy by ignoring her. Nancy's mother wanted Nancy to be at her wedding. Nancy's problem: How was she to handle her grandparents?

As I listened to Nancy speak, I was surprised. Grandparents, no matter what they were like as parents, usually in my experience come through for their grandchildren. Grandparenting is a very special relationship in which idealization, doting and spoiling are to be expected. The behavior of Nancy's grandparents *was not* to be expected.

However seventeen-year-old Lisa was not surprised. She had been in the same spot with her grandparents. While I struggled silently with my own rage at these self-centered grandparents, Lisa advised Nancy with an astounding wisdom and grace.

"I decided," said Lisa, as she described her own preparations for her mother's second marriage, "that the best thing I could do in these circumstances was to look as good as I could and to act as good as I could. There was no point in trying to get back at them by ignoring them or making a scene at the wedding. All that would do would make me look bad and convince them they were right about how awful I was. Making a scene would also hurt my mother on her special day and I didn't want to do that. So I planned it all out in advance. I even rehearsed it with my boyfriend. The best way of getting back was to look great, to be gracious, polite, sweet and pretty. And I was! I looked great. I acted great. I still believe it was the best thing I could have done under the circumstances."

I silently agreed. I silently wondered how she called forth such wisdom at such an early age. I also felt terribly sad that she had to be so old and look so good while still so very young.

Caretaking

Children are often expected to perform adult tasks as the family strains more and more under the burden of the addiction. Tina's mother abused tranquilizers all during Tina's childhood. The situation was tolerable for the children until their parents separated, at which point her mother rapidly abdicated almost entirely her role as caretaker of the children. "From the time I was about twelve," Tina reports, "Mom stopped doing everything." Tina had a younger sister and an older brother. At first her brother became their mother's main support. Within a year he had found a reason to leave home and the two girls were left to market, cook and clean. "We took care of each other because Mom just sat in her room all day feeling sorry for herself."

Mary's father was alcoholic and her mother felt overwhelmed by her five children, full-time job (which often provided the only income the family had), and unreliable alcoholic husband. She expected Mary to do most of the housework. Frequently Mary had no time for her homework because it took her so long to take care of the house. It was often ten o'clock at night before she had finished the dinner dishes and cleaned up the kitchen. She was never allowed to go out and play until all the household chores were completed. This meant that she almost never went out to play, thus robbing Mary of another important part of her childhood. Many adults recalling a childhood of alcoholism are painfully aware of this loss.

Play

Said one young man, a twenty-five-year-old rugged and often inarticulate construction worker, "I never had a childhood. I was always taking care of my mother. I never got a chance to play. Now, when I walk past a playground, I stop and watch the children play. Sometimes I cry."

Play is a child's work. It is a vital part of a child's life, used by the child to work on developmental tasks and to get some of the sustenance needed to lead a healthy life. Children use play to relieve tension, to work out problems and to act out their fantasies and wishes. Games, competition and play acting are all ways to learn more about the self and to enrich one's sense of the self. Being cheated of this experience impoverishes children.

Adults also need to play. For those adults who had to sacrifice this important part of their childhood to the needs of the family, play becomes lost to them unless they make a conscious effort to retrieve it. The construction worker admitted that it was almost impossible for him to relax and that he became uncomfortable around adults who were playful and having a good time. He left his first Al-Anon meeting because he was uncomfortable with the laughter and relaxed atmosphere he found there. He felt that if something was not serious it could not be worthwhile. Even when he engages in sports, he is so serious that he finds no joy in the game. He knew something was missing; his tears told him that. What was missing eluded him because he never knew it. This lack of playtime may be as serious and significant a loss in the lives of children of alcoholism as the more obvious losses these children sustain.

The Child As Pseudo-Spouse

Not only do children act as parents to their own parents, but at times they are expected to act as spouses. Incest, the most extreme boundary violation, is not a rare phenomenon in alcoholic families. There are also less obvious, less dramatic intrusions of such boundaries. Ellen's father often expected her to accompany him to his favorite bar because his wife would not. This put Ellen in a difficult position. Her father was fun to be with when he drank and she was flattered when he showered her with so much attention. She also knew that he was not supposed to drink and that going with him made her a partner in his "crime." The simple act of accompanying her father was not a simple act at all. It left her feeling both pleased and guilty at the same time. In addition, she knew that her mother would grill her when they arrived home about what had happened. This put Ellen in the middle of her parents' conflict. She became both accomplice and betrayer. Guilt became her unwelcome companion as she struggled with these equally unacceptable positions and found herself playing each one.

There is still more to add to the confusion and complexity of Ellen's dilemma. Ellen's mother would not accompany her husband on his drinking jaunts because she so vehemently disapproved of his drinking. Why then did she give Ellen tacit approval to accompany her father "to keep an eye on him?" Not only was Ellen's mother using her, but she was also communicating that Ellen must not recognize this. These were strange and paradoxical messages.

Kate, whose father expected her to protect the younger children from their alcoholic mother's violence, also was treated more like the

father's spouse than his own wife. Even while Kate rebelled inwardly
at what he was asking her to do, she was inwardly flattered. She
sympathized with this brave, overburdened, but well-intentioned
man and assumed the role of her father's partner with as much pride
as reluctance. This triumph over her mother would also leave Kate
filled with a guilt she might not understand or recognize but one that
would affect her in both present and future relationships.

Generational boundaries may not be the only ones blurred or
compromised. Danny reported that because he felt incapable of
making the adult decisions thrust upon him early in his life, he
would use his two younger brothers to give him the strength he
needed. He never made a decision without having them with him,
even though he was usually the one who worked out the solution.
If he came home after school and found his mother in trouble, he
would run through the neighborhood collecting his brothers so
that he could discuss with them what to do. He reported feeling
incomplete without them but whole when the three of them were
together. Interpersonal boundaries blurred for Danny as he felt
frequently fused with his two brothers.

Siblings

Special attention should be paid to the role of siblings in an
alcoholic family. Relationships among brothers and sisters may be
particularly difficult for a variety of reasons. The fact that some
siblings parent other siblings complicates and intensifies their
feelings about each other. The normal competitiveness and
jealousies that occur among siblings may not get worked out
properly because the parental system, which should provide
guidance and set limits in the acting out of these conflicts, may be
under such stress that it adds to the problems rather than helps
resolve them. The blurring of personal boundaries to gather and
consolidate strength as exemplified by Danny may further intensify
and complicate the relationships. Adult children of alcoholics often
find that they and their siblings have very different perceptions of
their childhood and their parents' roles in their lives. Although all
children have different experiences with their parents based on
sex, age, role in the family, personality, etc., children of alcoholism
find it particularly painful to tolerate the differences in perceptions
among siblings. Some of this has to do with the role of denial in the
alcoholic family and the use of various defenses to survive the
onslaught of the parental alcoholism. Some of it may also have to

do with the tremendous importance that siblings have for each other. Adult siblings who find they take a position different from their brothers and sisters, for example, insisting that one parent was alcoholic while others deny this, fear (and sometimes with good reason) that they will be abandoned by the other siblings. When this is combined with the powerful self-doubting that frequently plagues children of alcoholism, the lack of agreement may feel like an invalidation of one's perceptions and childhood experiences. This often is experienced not only as the loss of a loved one, but also as a loss of part of the self.

Privacy

Invasion of privacy is another violation of personal boundaries. People remember mail being opened, phone calls being listened to surreptitiously, closets and drawers being searched or disrupted, and even pets being destroyed or given away during a parent's drunken rage. These are more common than rare occurrences in alcoholic families. These are all violations of personal boundaries. Children are left feeling there is nothing they can call their own; nothing is safe from the random destructiveness or intrusion by insensitive and irrational parents. This vulnerability reinforces the feeling of being victims in a world over which they have no control, not even of their most private and cherished possessions.

Tina reported that she felt as if her mother took over even her feelings. After her parents divorced, her mother deluged her with ugly stories and complaints about her father. She would become outraged if Tina did not show the proper sympathy for her. Her mother would accuse Tina of taking her father's side and being disloyal to her. Tina admitted that she stopped knowing what her true feelings about her father really were and what feelings she assumed to placate her mother. Similar to Tina, Audrey reported a feeling of invasion of her inner life as well as her possessions. Audrey became alcoholic, "just like my mother," she mused sadly. The youngest of three girls, she was ten when her father died. Her mother soon began drinking alcoholically. Already invasive and controlling, the mother turned her attention more and more to her children with her husband gone. "After my father died it was like she merged with me," Audrey reported. She paused, her eyes tortured, and then proceeded, "I'm thirty-one years old, married and I've never had anything I can call my own. My mother took over everything. First she picked out my clothes and controlled who my friends were. Later she picked out the furniture in my home and interfered in my marriage. It seemed like she took over everything: my marriage and my home. I never knew where she ended and I began."

Alliances And Loyalties

In most of these examples, not only are roles reversed but unhealthy alliances are formed in the process. Kate was asked to ally with her father against her mother. Jeremy and Tina were expected to ally with mother against father. Eli, whose mother protected his father from disclosure in the emergency room, perceived this as an alliance to cover up the abuse of his sister, an unholy alliance of mother with father in which he also was expected to collude.

Loyalties almost always result in unresolvable conflicts for children who are expected by parents or circumstance to pick a side, to declare a loyalty that will make them ultimately disloyal to someone else. This issue is even more amplified if there is a divorce or separation.

Divorce

Jamie is ten years old. His parents have been divorced since he was a toddler but they continue to do battle with one another via child support and visitation rights. Their anger and resentment with each other remain unabated despite the years of separation. Jamie reports that he feels forever caught in the crossfire of this bitter battle between his parents. Showing a wisdom that should be beyond him he remarks, "They fight through me. My mother, she's obvious. When she drinks she wakes me up in the middle of the night to tell me how mean my father is. She shows me all the bills she can't pay because he won't give her enough money. My father doesn't do those things. He doesn't talk about her. But he uses me to get to her too. I don't think he knows he does it, though."

His fifteen-year-old sister Alison describes the ongoing battles she engages in with her mother as Alison feels compelled to side with her father. Although this is not an unusual position for a teenage girl, it is tremendously complicated for Alison because of her mother's alcoholism and the conflicts between her parents that encourage Alison to perpetuate rather than resolve her conflicts with her mother.

Jamie often finds himself in the middle of those fights also. As Alison pauses, Jamie shakes his head and says, "It's like I'm in a war all the time." He then goes on to elaborate how this war has two fronts, the one between his mother and father and the other between his mother and sister. Each one pulls at his loyalties, expects his support and experiences neutrality or positions other than what each of them wants as personal affronts. In addition, Jamie is not only victim and passive protagonist in this "war story," he is quite capable of taking the first shot in one of the endless rounds of the ongoing battle.

Such dynamics are not uncommon when divorce disrupts a family; they become even more difficult for a child to manage when one parent, in this case the mother, is also alcoholic. Alliances and loyalties, already compromised and strained to the breaking point because of the addiction, become even more stressed by separation and divorce. The ambivalence toward the parents that is so intense and complicated by the alcoholism makes it even more difficult for children then to come to grips with their ambivalent feelings about separation and divorce.

Frequently the parents who are so caught up in their own lives, do little to ease the situation for the children. Jamie's parents, both well-educated and even somewhat psychologically oriented, knew that it was detrimental for the children to be pawns in their vengeful chess game. However the parents kept drawing the children in, asking them at whose house they wanted to stay or withholding money from the children for important services in their unrelenting attempts to hurt each other.

Custody

Ellie and Kira also have an alcoholic mother. Their parents engaged in a lengthy and bitter divorce, with custody of the children a major source of conflict. While the girls were still living with their mother, they were taken to court and told to choose with whom they wanted to live. The mother's alcoholism by that point had her nearly out of control and unable to care for them adequately. They chose their father. When they talk about it, they are very apologetic, defensive and seemingly reasonable about a decision that obviously caused them great discomfort. Developmentally, it was a terrible time for them to have to make such a choice. Their mother's untreated alcoholism and the parents' unresolved conflicts tremendously complicated the girls' feelings about their mother and their own identities as young women.

They continue to maintain a relationship with their mother that is exceedingly complex. Their father, whether out of genuine concern for the girls' well-being and safety or from continuing anger at his ex-wife, manipulates the visitation rights and tries to minimize the amount of time the girls have to see their mother. The mother "retaliates" by getting drunk while the girls are there and then drives them back to their father's, making a scene in front of his house that disturbs the neighbors and leaves the girls feeling embarrassed and humiliated. This situation complicates the girls' feelings about their mother. They seem aware of the fact that they are pawns in the ongoing conflicts between their parents and that the love and attention they receive is conditional and somehow related to the parents' battles. However they do not acknowledge this and change the subject when discussion gets too close to this fact. This may be out of loyalty to the parents, or it may reflect their inability to manage the complexity and contradictions inherent in the situation. In either case, being unable to talk about it also means that they cannot lessen the devastation of its impact upon them.

The Threat Of Divorce

Greg's parents never divorced. But divorce was nevertheless an ongoing issue in the family. Greg's mother continually blamed her children for her inability to leave her alcoholic husband. She let the children know repeatedly how miserable she was with their father and how she would have divorced him if it had not been for them. This put the children in a terrible bind. They wanted and at the same time did not want the parents to separate. They felt both relieved and guilty when the parents did not, but above all, they somehow felt responsible for the misery of their parents.

Children getting caught in the conflicts of parents is not unique to children of alcoholism. However the loosening of defenses that results from either the drinking or the stresses of living with an alcoholic may make parents in an alcoholic family less likely to properly protect the children from these impossible positions. Alcohol loosens tongues and lowers inhibitions. Under the influence of alcohol people will say things they would not say in more sober circumstances. The nondrinking parent may find the pressures of the alcoholism having an equally regressive and disinhibiting effect. Children become the victims of this lack of inhibition and are then forced to make choices they should not have to make; take sides when they should not be taking sides;

assume guilt when they are innocent and accept responsibilities that are well beyond their capacities.

The very purpose of a family, the protection and sustenance of its members and particularly the nurturing and rearing of its children, breaks down if alcoholism is allowed to intrude on the family structures. These structures, so vital for a child's healthy growth and development, do not in such cases serve the child's needs. Instead these structures are used to support the alcoholism. Families organized around an addiction rather than around the nurturing of its members do not promote healthy growth of their members. Roles and boundaries become compromised and distorted; alliances and loyalties are misdirected; and, most tragic of all, children are often left to raise themselves.

Silence

CHAPTER 3

The Elephant In The Living Room

In thinking about communication in an alcoholic family a story comes to mind. It is a book written for children entitled *The Elephant in the Living Room*. The story describes metaphorically the effects of living with alcoholism. For the child this is like living in a very small house with a huge elephant planted firmly in the middle of the living room. In order for members of the family to pass from one room to another they must go through the living room and thus squeeze around this enormous elephant that dwarfs the small room. And nobody ever talks about it! Everybody squeezes around the elephant and accommodates the elephant but no one ever talks about the elephant. No one even acknowledges that the elephant is there. It controls everybody's life by the enormity of its presence, but still no one admits that the elephant exists. What a vivid description of alcoholic denial and its effects on communication.

I call this chapter "Silence" because it seems more descriptive of the communication that occurs in an alcoholic family than does the word communication. As patterns in an alcoholic family are examined, one comes face to face with paradox, with contradiction, with illusion. And so the silence. For silence speaks louder and sometimes truer than speech in families of alcoholism. It certainly speaks with more power.

The Lack Of Explanations

Eli lived with silence, the silence of what was not said and what was not talked about, the silence of the elephant in the living room. The word alcoholic was never used to describe Eli's father, to explain his mood swings and sudden violence. This lack of labeling and explanation contributes to the confusion frequently described by Eli and other adult children of alcoholics.

Without explanations there can be no meanings attached to important parental behaviors, behaviors that have profound effects on a child's life (such as Eli's father pushing Eli's sister down a flight of stairs) but for which there is no apparent, rational or understandable reason. When no explanations are given for such behaviors, children attach their own meanings. This often means they blame themselves for their parents' behavior. This in turn can leave them with a life-long sense of guilt that becomes generalized to many aspects of their own behavior and leaves them feeling guilty in any situation in which they feel powerless or out of control.

The lack of an explanation for significant behavior can also lead children to perceive the world as irrational and arbitrary before they are developmentally ready to deal with such a concept. Parents usually help children with difficult ideas, often by giving them explanations that may not be accurate from an adult perspective (because they are too simple) but that are understandable and therefore usable for the child. When it comes to a parent's alcoholism and the terrible things that may occur because of it, this does not happen. Cause and effect are not connected to these important events. As a result the children develop a vision of a world in which they have no understanding and no control. This further entrenches the feeling that they are helpless victims in an arbitrary and irrational universe.

Deceptiveness Of Speech

There is another dimension to the silence for Eli. This has to do with deception. Remember that Eli's sister had to be rushed to the hospital for injuries sustained when her father threw her down a flight of stairs. Eli reported that his father lied to the emergency room personnel, telling them his daughter had fallen off a chair. And then Eli said, "My mother was there, too. She didn't say a word. But she knew. And I knew, too." The silence becomes a conspiracy to deceive. Even his mother, who does not drink, who puts great value on honesty and whom he looks up to and respects, conspires by her silence to keep the truth hidden about his sister. Worst of all, he implies by his tortured look as he stops speaking, Eli too becomes a co-conspirator, an unwilling but silent co-conspirator.

Not only silence, but also speech becomes conveyor of deception. Eli's father blatantly lied to cover up his own misbehavior. Carl also received a deceitful message from his mother. When Carl saw his father passed out on the living room sofa, he went racing, terrified, to tell his mother. She insisted his father was merely sleeping. Carl sensed the difference, knowing this was not the same as his father's appearance when simply asleep. Carl's mother had blurred the truth by her unthinking attempt to reassure Carl. Rather than reassuring, it increased Carl's anxiety, for he was then faced with opposing perceptions. He had to decide whose version he was to trust — his mother's or his own.

This is an impossible dilemma for a child to resolve. If he affirms his own perceptions he implies his mother is lying. This would feel like great disloyalty because his mother puts a high value on the truth. If he chooses to support his mother's verbal interpretation, then he cannot trust his own perceptions. The profound doubting that so frequently plagues Carl may have arisen from just such scenes as he has here described.

Denial, rationalization and minimization are all defenses used in great abundance by the alcoholic and often by the family. It is important to remember that defenses are not under one's conscious control; they are neither deliberately chosen nor consciously applied. People are unaware when they are using defense mechanisms. The lack of awareness is part of the protective nature of a defense. This lack of awareness spares the individual knowledge that would be uncomfortable or provoke anxiety. The unconscious nature of defenses increases the confusion for the child who is experiencing the parents' use of denial, rationalization, avoidance or minimization because the parent seems neither ambivalent nor purposely deceptive when distorting the truth. Yet most children are aware to some degree that what they are being told is not necessarily the truth. This creates for the child who listens the notion that speech is contaminated, not to be trusted and not a reflection of the truth.

The Devaluation Of Speech

Alcoholic parents often make promises in the rosy glow of intoxication that they have no memory of the next day. Children do not connect those broken promises with an alcoholic blackout (loss of memory but not consciousness during heavy drinking) because they do not know what an alcoholic blackout is. At other times promises may be kept. This inconsistency is particularly damaging for children still entertaining hope that promises will be kept. Children learn not to trust their own hope and not to trust that promises will be kept because so frequently they are broken. A painful cycle of hopeful anticipation and bitter disappointment is thus set in motion; again the vehicle is speech.

The co-dependent parent also uses speech in ways that are damaging to the child. Accusations, hysterical threats and manipulation are frantic attempts to control the alcoholic's drinking. Children hear threats that the co-dependent parent plans to leave the alcoholic. This will frighten the children if they take those threats literally and seriously. Hearing them repeated and never carried through may continue to raise anxiety but also will lessen the value the child puts on the integrity of speech. Repeated accusations and denials, whether related to actual drinking or to behavior connected to the drinking, also create grave doubts about the value of communication in children who are an unwilling audience to such verbal exchanges. Broken promises, hysterical threats and accusations all contribute to the sense that speech is more to be feared and guarded against than to be used to express feelings and concerns, to ask questions, to test impressions and perceptions and get reliable feedback. If speech is used to break promises, to make angry threats and to argue endlessly without resolving conflicts, then speech is not a tool for problem solving. Speech may in fact *create* problems rather than lead to their resolution. Said one young man, "I never listen to what people say to me. I watch their faces, their bodies. That's why I like my dog so much. I can always tell where he's at. He can't talk so he can't lie." Thus, silence seems preferable.

Prohibitions To Speech

The silence surrounding the behavior is also a mixed and powerful message. For Eli the silence conveys the prohibition to speak about the events most important in his life, the events most surrounded by feelings. The silence is used to cover up, to protect his father's alcoholic drinking. Because it is so laden with indescribable emotions it takes on a power hard to diffuse.

Silence takes many forms. It is the tense lines around a mother's mouth as she wordlessly prepares breakfast to the sounds of banging pots and slamming cabinet doors. The silence both avoids and encapsulates the harsh words the child heard pass between his parents moments earlier. He dare not ask questions when his mother looks so tense. This is another silence the child comes to know. It is the lift of an eyebrow, the frown on a face or the turning away when a child asks a question about the drinking, the fighting or the tears. Silence is a powerful prohibition, an unspoken command not to speak, not to voice feelings and not to question confusing events. Chatter around inconsequential events is acceptable and even desirable. The truly important events demand silence.

Silence is the stifled cry in a child's throat as she sits in a car beside her inebriated mother and the car swerves dangerously, barely missing an oncoming car. Even before she gets in the car, the little girl can tell that her mother has been drinking. She hates to drive with her mother when she's drunk. But she says nothing, and gets into the car quietly. If she speaks about her mother's condition or shows fear or anxiety as her mother goes speeding away, her mother not only will drive carelessly but she also will be angry and perhaps drive even more aggressively and recklessly. Instead the little girl sits quietly, only her white knuckles indicating the tension she is feeling. Her silence surrounds the screeching of the brakes and the skidding of the tires. The silence protects her from her mother's wrath but also isolates her, prevents her from expressing her fear and getting comfort, relief or feedback to help her sort out the complicated feelings such an experience evokes.

Silence is the stillness of peace in the middle of the night suddenly shattered by the sounds of the liquor cabinet opening, ice jangling in a glass and then liquid being poured. There is more silence, this time not peaceful as the child waits in tense anticipation. Then that uneasy silence is broken by voices first whispering, next rising and then shouting, followed by the sounds of broken glass and a slamming front door. Then again the silence returns, no longer peaceful but oppressive and frightening. This is the silence that disrupts sleep rather than promotes it, that leads to fitful tossing and turning, to nightmares and to waking up still tired and irritable rather than well-rested and refreshed.

The Power Of Silence

There can be another aspect to the silence. The riches of silence may never be discovered by people who experience silence as a threat and as the precursor to violence or abandonment. One must surround oneself with quiet to contemplate and be reflective. People who are comfortable with each other can be together in silence, reinforcing the closeness and supporting the intimacy rather than preventing it. Silence can sustain and nurture. It allows one to appreciate the riches of the inner life and to value the self as the source of those riches. It also enables one to recognize the self as the source of the inner peace that can come through silence. Silence can lead to serenity when one is comfortable being alone with oneself and one's quietness.

Children of alcoholism may never know this positive side of the silence. Only knowing silence as a defense, as a barrier between people and as an obstacle to truth is a real loss. Paradoxically, losses may also result from breaking the silence of the alcoholic family.

Breaking And Maintaining The Silence

Alcoholism depends on the silence that surrounds it. Silence keeps the alcoholism secret and unconfronted. The price for breaking that silence is dear. It is like breaking a taboo, which is all the more threatening because it is an unwritten, unverbalized taboo. With the breaking comes anxiety, guilt and a tremendous sense of disloyalty. For anything of importance that can be said will somehow implicate the parents and will sound and feel like blame, even when it is only description. Blame is particularly to be guarded against because it risks unleashing a rage that might be uncontrollable.

Breaking the silence poses another risk. Siblings growing up in the same household and at the same time often have very different impressions of what is happening in the household. Some use more denial than others. Some feel particularly strong loyalties to one parent and let these loyalties color their perceptions of what is happening. To speak to one another risks exposing the different perceptions. This may feel too threatening in a home where the parents' messages to the children are already contradictory and confusing. Differences of opinion also cause rifts within the sibling system when the need to maintain certain perceptions or certain defense mechanisms is unconsciously linked to survival. At the same time, self-doubt makes it difficult to take a stand in opposition to the others. It is easier and safer not to say anything. People frequently describe sharing the same bedroom with a sister or brother, listening nightly to parents arguing or being violent and never discussing this with the sibling in the next bed, at the time of the events or later. Many people also describe that when they have attempted to discuss the past with a sibling, they find radical differences in perception occurring. Often the outcome is just what they had feared the most: siblings who stop talking to each other and even cut off all contact with each other rather than tolerate the differences they discover in their memories or their interpretations of the past.

But the price for maintaining the silence is also dear. Silence isolates. It intensifies the feeling that one is different from others since there can be no one with whom to compare notes, to share the feelings. Silence prevents common bonds from developing between people sharing similar experiences. It prevents feedback to correct misimpressions, distortions in thinking and false assumptions, all so prevalent in families of alcoholism. Silence cripples. It prevents talking about difficult things as a way to achieve mastery over them. Silence stifles. It prevents having a safe outlet for strong feelings. It may even prevent learning how to identify and name feelings. Not being able to identify one's feelings makes one a stranger even to oneself. Silence stifles. It cripples. It isolates.

The Caretaker
Part I

Who is taking care of whom and how is an ongoing and often never resolved problem in a family organized around an addiction. Although this was examined in Chapter 2, "Family Life: Compromised Structures" (the section on role reversal), it exerts such a major influence on the development of the child that it needs to be further described as a separate phenomenon. Issues around caretaking have many faces.

Taking Care Of The Addiction

Sally is three years old. I met her when her mother brought her to an interview she had scheduled with me. Sally's father was hospitalized for treatment of his poly-drug abuse and I was meeting with Ann, Sally's mother, to assess the family situation and needs for treatment. Ann was also poly-drug addicted and the focus of the interview was to be getting Ann into inpatient treatment for herself.

It was immediately apparent that Ann knew how to take care of Sally in some ways. Sally was well-scrubbed from head to toe and her sandy-brown, shoulder-length hair was neatly combed. She was appropriately dressed for her age in a simple, attractive pink and white striped sunsuit with matching pink and white striped socks and white shoes. However, she was slight of frame (fragile-looking rather than delicate) and there was a pallor to her skin that made her look unhealthy. She had large, dark somber eyes. Her face too had a serious expression and she looked, despite the age-appropriate dress, like a very old woman.

I gave Sally a coloring book and crayons to occupy her and she colored quietly while I talked to her mother. She was quiet for longer than I would have expected of a three-year-old. After quite some time she quietly closed the book, put the crayons neatly back in the box and then cautiously began to explore my office. Rather quickly she squeezed between the wall and a large arm chair that her mother was sitting in, hidden from view except for an occasional tiny hand reaching out to touch a bouquet of dried flowers sitting next to the chair.

Ann expressed ambivalence about going into treatment for herself but was basically agreeable to the idea. As the specifics of time and place were discussed, she talked about how difficult it was to set any limits on her drug use. Something she said prompted me to emphasize that it would be necessary for her to stop *all* drug and alcohol use, not only her drugs of choice. It was the most direct and confronting I had been with her during the interview.

Suddenly Sally was standing next to her mother, slightly in front of her and directly facing me, as if subtly guarding her mother from my intervention. Looking directly at me, her voice firm and strong, she very intently and intensely said, "I can make her stop using. I can make her stop."

So tiny, so frail-looking was this three-year-old, yet her voice seemed to fill the room, her affirmation of her mission dwarfed her mother and me. I felt silenced, off-guard and inadequate in the presence of the burden she so heroically assumed. In an awkward attempt to say something helpful to her I leaned forward and very gently said, "You can't make your mother stop using, Sally. No one can do that." She shook her head sternly, raised her voice a little more, took on the tone of a scolding mother and replied, "Yes I can. I can make her stop." She turned her head toward her mother at that point. She did not move her hands, but it seemed as if she were shaking a finger at her mother as she continued, "I tell her all the time she has to stop."

At that point her mother leaned over and kissed her little girl and said, "No, Sally, you can't make me stop. Only I can make me stop. But it doesn't mean I don't love you." Sally looked straight through her mother. Whether she even heard either of us was unclear. Certainly, she did not attend to what we said, did not absorb it or take it seriously. She continued to stand protectively and slightly in front of her mother through the rest of the interview, alert not for what I would say to her, but for any possible further confrontation of her mother.

Sally, at age three, is already taking care of her mother and protecting her from suspected harm or attack. In her own mind she has taken charge of her mother's addiction and has assumed responsibility for controlling it. "I can make her stop," was said stridently, almost fiercely, with an intensity of determination that enlarged her, aged her and made her unreachable. If Sally takes the control of her mother's addiction as her life-long mission, as some children do, and if she then connects her self-esteem and her identity with that mission, as some children do, then Sally undertakes the impossible. Her only reward will be an ongoing sense of failure and no sense of herself as a separate human being apart from her mother and her mission to cure her mother. If all achievements are linked to achieving sobriety for her mother, as happens with some children, then no achievement will bring with it satisfaction or a feeling of accomplishment. Sally will always have failed because she never achieved the one goal she set for herself — her mother's sobriety. Even if her mother eventually decides to stop using drugs, the achievement will be her own, not Sally's. No matter what Sally does, she can never do what she most desires to do, and living with that will continuously erode her self-esteem.

Clearly, Sally's mother loved her daughter and knew how to take care of her. She groomed her well and spoke to her with sensitivity and affection. But I called Ann around ten o'clock one morning to set up an appointment. Her voice was heavy with sleep and her speech slurred by more than sleep, it seemed. I remember wondering, after the call, whether I should call back later in the day to be sure she remembered our call. I wonder, at such times, how attentive she could be to Sally. What happens at that time of day if Sally gets hungry or scared or lonely? Can her mother be available to her then?

In addition to living by the dictates of her addiction, Sally's mother also has to cope with the stresses of living with a drug-addicted husband. Ann reported that she was alienated from her own family and her husband's family. When asked where she received support for herself, she admitted that she had no resources of her own. She had become increasingly isolated as the addiction had progressed. She also had become increasingly preoccupied with the addictions that control the family. How attentive can she be to Sally?

Certainly Sally seems to be more concerned about her mother than about herself, which is unusual for a three-year-old. Although she is too young to talk about these things, her behavior speaks eloquently. Sally protects her mother as she stands by her side. Sally makes no demands on her mother as she colors quietly for too long and as she tidies the crayons and coloring book when she finishes with them. She gives the impression as she half-scolds her mother when she says, "I tell her to stop all the time" that in some way Sally questions her mother's ability to care for herself. I wonder if Sally's appearance, the appearance of an old woman caught in a three-year-old body, may reflect this experience?

The Young Adolescent: Julie

I am reminded of another child I met several years ago, when her mother was hospitalized for alcoholism. Julie, a pretty, soft-spoken redhead, was fourteen years old. The oldest of six children in an upper-middle class family, Julie had already read a lot about alcoholism in attempts to understand her mother's long-standing, intractable disease. Julie insisted she knew that she neither caused nor could control her mother's alcoholism and even helped me to emphasize that point with her younger brothers and sisters. Julie also insisted her many successes in school gave her intrinsic satisfaction and were in no way connected to her mother's drinking.

One day, flushed with happiness and excitement, she rushed in to tell me that some of her poetry had been accepted for the school literary magazine. Her poetry was her most precious activity and her most personal. As we began to look at what the acceptance for the magazine meant to her, she admitted that perhaps, "If my poetry is good enough, my mother will be so proud of me she will stop drinking."

Julie had learned, as would Sally eventually, that she could not simply tell her mother to stop drinking and expect her mother to comply. The attempts to control the alcoholism, therefore, had gone underground where even Julie did not recognize them. They were expressed now through Julie's achievements. She unconsciously told herself, "If I am good enough, smart enough or clever enough, I'll find a way to cure my mother." Even this most personal activity that Julie had identified as her own and in no way connected to her family, is unconsciously used by Julie in the service of her mother's alcoholism. The feeling of triumph will soon fade when her hidden agenda is not met, when recognition of her poetry does not bring about a cure for her mother. No matter how successful she becomes the success will not give her sustained pleasure, nor will it increase her self-esteem because that is linked to curing her mother's alcoholic drinking. And that she will never do.

The Older Adolescent: Peter

Some children, like Julie, attempt to cure their parent through achievement: academic success, excellence in sports or some other significant area in their lives for which they manage to receive recognition from others. Other children, with similar goals, may take an opposite approach. By getting into trouble in school, at home or in the community, they distract the parents from their own problems. This supports the parents' denial of the alcoholism as they rush to tend to a troubled child. It seems easier to face the child's misbehavior than the parent's drinking. This too is caretaking for it protects the parents from what the child senses they are not able to face.

Peter was such a child. I met him when his mother was hospitalized for a drug addiction that had started when Peter was just a little boy. Peter's father, a lawyer, soon tired of his wife's repeated and unsuccessful attempts to get help and left the family. By then Peter was already getting into trouble. He was arrested for stealing cars at age fifteen. He was in and out of homes for delinquent boys, always returning to his mother. When I met him he was nineteen and looked every inch the rebellious adolescent. With uncombed hair hanging down to his shoulders, a dirty T-shirt, leather jacket and unshaven face, I half expected to see a motorcycle parked outside my office door.

He swaggered in and I offered him my hand, asking as I did, "How are you, Peter?" As he shook my hand he straightened, assumed an air of solemn gravity and in a deep voice replied, "More important, how is my mother?" He sounded like a concerned father asking about a troublesome child. Despite his guardedness with me and his tendency to grandstand about his delinquent behavior, it was clear he worried about his mother, tried to monitor her drug use and at times interrupted his own drug abuse in attempts to get hers under control. He described how they alternated taking care of each other and attempted to control each other's addiction. As he talked, the bravado diminished and beneath it was revealed not only a tenderness and genuine concern for his mother but also a determination to cure her that equalled

Sally's and Julie's determination. His desire however, (perhaps because he was older and therefore exposed to the addiction for longer) was tinged with a cynicism and despair that had not been manifested in the younger children.

Taking Care Of The Family

The Adult: Alicia

Alicia is thirty-seven years old. She was first described as the twelve-year-old who trudged three miles through the snow, her siblings in tow, so they could spend Christmas with her friend's family. Their parents had gone out "celebrating" the night before and left the children alone. When her older brother got into difficulty in school, Alicia met with the principal because her parents did not. She gave her sister a birthday party because, again, her parents did not. She now admits that she took on more responsibility than she should have. "I felt older as a kid than I do now."

One can speculate as to whether her parents would have taken better care of the children if Alicia had not taken over so quickly. Had the parents' neglect been more apparent it might have come to the attention of extended family or school authorities. Alicia may have inadvertently supported her parents' denial by covering up their inadequacies as parents while she parented herself and her siblings. One can also speculate on where her need to be a caretaker arose and on whether this caretaking was ultimately a way of taking care of herself. What needs no speculation, what is undeniably clear is the felt need of a twelve-year-old to assume responsibilities beyond her years and capacities.

When asked to describe her parents she remembered each as unavailable. Her father was violent and verbally abusive when drunk, or distant, cold and withdrawn when not drinking. "When sober, he didn't exist," is the way she described his lack of emotional involvement with the family.

On the other hand, she described her mother as a "victim" who also assumed different roles when drinking and not drinking. When drinking along with her husband she was irresponsible. She would stay out all night with Alicia's father, leaving the children home alone and unattended. Or she would arrive home drunk in the middle of the night, along with her husband and their friends. She would then wake the children from a deep sleep to show them off for their inebriated guests. When not drinking, her mother went to the other extreme and was "super-responsible." It sounded as if there was a quality of martyr and atoner for past sins in this behavior that made it as unmodulated and inattentive to the children's true needs as the "irresponsible" behavior. Corroborating this Alicia remarked, "They were both absent a lot, whether there or not."

She reflects for a minute and then continues, "I had so little control over so much . . ." and then goes on to describe how issues of control destroyed her marriage and continue to plague her in subsequent relationships. Although she does not elaborate in regard to her childhood, it seems obvious that these issues were as complicated, confusing and contradictory as the experiences of Eli and Carl. For Eli and Carl the alcoholism itself was in question. For Alicia, "Who takes care of whom," and as a result, "Who controls what?" are elusive, not clearly evident, not rationally or predictably determined. To an observer, it is clear that a ten- or twelve-year-old cannot keep a family together and cannot take over adequately the functions of a mother and father. But to twelve-year-old Alicia, who *did* manage to salvage some vestige of a Christmas celebration, who *did* make a party for her little sister, who *did* talk to the school principal, there was at least the *appearance* of control. To the observer, the reason for the desperate and ongoing need for control is apparent and resides in the lack of actual control this child had over the chaos and crisis caused by her parents' alcoholism. Again, Alicia corroborates, "I never felt scared; I felt responsible."

There is another facet to this phenomenon. Although Alicia became very proficient at taking care of others, she was not nearly as good at taking care of herself. Tuned always to the needs of others she was far less attuned to herself and was often at a loss to identify her own needs or to see that they were met. She was also less likely to look to others for help even when that might be appropriate. Taking care of others may have become the *only* way that Alicia knew to take care of herself. She took care of her brother and sister because her parents did not. She took care of them as a way of taking care of herself, again because her parents did not. She took care of herself, her brother and her sister as a way of taking care of parents who clearly did not take care of themselves. It is important to note the intensity of the experience. Alicia described her caretaking in a driven manner that reminds me of Sally as she stared intently at me and told me how she could make her mother stop using drugs.

Use Of The Self As Caretaker

Jamie is ten years old. He is the child described earlier as caught in an endless battle between his warring, divorced parents. Jamie does not look or act like a caretaker. The younger of two children of an alcoholic mother, he usually acts like the baby of the family. He is slight of frame, wiry and energetic. Large dark eyes dominate a pale, freckled face that is sometimes impish and sometimes serious. He looks no more than eight years old. As I offer him and his fifteen-year-old sister Alison cookies before we begin our interview his sister turns them down as beneath her dignity to so indulge. Jamie, however, politely but greedily snatches up as many as his small hands can hold. As he sits down in an over-stuffed chair in my office his size is accentuated: he seems to get lost in the chair, making him look even younger. He carefully arranges his cookies on the table next to him, piling them up much the way a younger child would stack a pile of building blocks.

Then he begins to speak. Gone, suddenly, is the eight or ten year old. Instead a very wise adult seems to be talking. He describes the conflicted loyalties in the family with a sophistication that belongs to a family therapist. He describes the overt but also the covert battles being waged almost daily between his mother and father, his mother and sister and his sister and himself. He details the dire consequences for himself each time he is sucked into an alliance with one person as it affects his relationship with the other two. He pauses for a moment, looking very old, and reflecting a sadness and an understanding of his parents' behavior that should be well beyond his years.

And then suddenly there is an impish gleam in his eyes as he describes his childish way of retaliating against his sister when he is angry at her or the way he has learned to tease and upset her. A fleeting look of triumph in his eyes he then quickly turns and attacks his pile of cookies. Crumbs fly this way and that as he squirms restlessly in his chair now looking more like a five- or six-year-old. The wise old man and the fidgety young child keep alternating throughout the interview.

Jamie is here exhibiting a more subtle form of caretaking. He is chameleon-like. He has an uncanny ability to sense what is expected of him and to give it. He describes family dynamics to the family therapist. He is an understanding, sympathetic listener to his mother as she pours out her tale of misery to him. He is the well-adjusted, athletic, good student and happy little boy his father wants him to be. Jamie takes care of people by being what they want him to be. As I watch Jamie alternate between wise old man and immature ten-year-old, watching me always out of the corner of his eye, I wonder if he is not also taking care of me, making sure I get the interview I want.

The
Inner Life

PART II

CHAPTER 5

Running Away

The Avoidance Of The Emotional Life

To avoid feeling when I was a kid, I would race down the highest hill standing up on my bike. Now, what can I do?

Megan, Age 22

Development Of Defense Mechanisms

Over time all people develop strategies for getting along in the world. Some of these strategies are consciously developed and consciously applied; others are unconscious. The latter are used automatically and instinctively much like the blinking of the eyes or a surge of adrenalin in the face of perceived danger. These unconscious coping techniques are called defense mechanisms and the foundations for their use are laid early in life. It is important to remember that everyone uses defense mechanisms. They are necessary at times for survival and at other times to ease anxiety and to make functioning more comfortable or more efficient. For example, a person facing a dangerous situation may do better if his fear is denied and he focuses instead on the skills he will need to get through the danger. It is common for people to suppress intense dislike of a powerful authority figure if there seems to be no other way to deal safely with such feelings. People spare themselves conscious awareness of feelings, thoughts or perceptions that might cause them shame or guilt; for example, jealousy or envy of a loved one or desires for revenge when hurt.

It is the extensiveness of their use and the flexibility with which defenses are used that determines how adaptive or maladaptive their use becomes and how much influence they exert over one's life. When defenses are applied excessively or too rigidly, when they compromise the ability to appraise and perceive realistically and accurately, when they interfere with productive decision-making, then they have become another problem rather than the solution to the problem.

When defense mechanisms are linked to survival, as happens with children who feel their survival is not secure, they become deeply entrenched, unquestioned and rigid. Mark when he ran away from home reflects the use of defense mechanisms that are typical in their over-use by children of alcoholism. The phrase "running away" is used here to characterize the cluster of defenses developed by such children who perceive life and the expression of feeling as a danger or threat to their very survival. Such defenses include: *avoidance* (of feelings, conflict and threatening situations); *isolation,* the separation of memory and the feelings attached to it; *projection,* the disowning of unacceptable feelings and their attribution to someone else; and *acting out,* the expression of conflict through behavior rather than dealing with it on a verbal and feeling level.

Mark's story is one of running away. In it he describes persevering through wind and rain and muddy fields and jumping into an icy river when he suddenly finds himself facing an oncoming train and there is no other way to escape. Despite these physical hardships, he keeps running, unwilling to return home. He is finally taken in by a friendly farm couple who give him dry clothes, hot food and a comfortable bed in exchange for his doing chores around the farm. He attempts to stay up all night so as not to be late for work his first day on the job. But overcome with fatigue, he falls asleep sometime near daybreak. Unbeknownst to him the couple let him sleep around the clock and when he discovers this, he is amazed by their kindness.

In his story about running away Mark does not describe the specifics of what he was trying to escape; he says only, "I couldn't stand the life there anymore." He does not elaborate. One can make assumptions if one looks at his choices. Instead of returning home he chooses an experience that threatens him with physical pain and peril, that is characterized by harsh climate and threats to his survival (an oncoming train and an icy river). The life he runs away from seems even worse because of his lack of reference to it and the silence that surrounds it. Later, Mark described some of those experiences. They were described sparingly with none of the detail he used to embellish his story of running away. What he said was that his father behaved erratically and violently on a regular basis. He remembered his father dragging him to bars, telling him he was "dumb" when he brought home average grades and hitting him with a board. There were times when he physically put himself between his mother and father to interrupt the father's violence toward the mother. And he remembers seeing his father put a revolver to his mother's head.

Such experiences help explain Mark's choice to keep running despite the physical discomforts because the life at home brought emotional as well as physical pain. Mark does not describe the emotional pain. At most, his voice takes on a tone of bitterness, but his words describe only the events and not his emotional responses to those events. Mark does not explain why he continued to run even when the running threatened grave danger and discomfort. However the intensity with which he told his story and the absolute determination to escape inform us of the importance of this act, the sense of running away being a truly critical choice for Mark.

It is also significant, given how important this experience has been, that Mark uses almost no feeling words in his story. The paucity of feelings is contrasted with the fullness and clarity of detail in his description of his environment. He describes in great detail the wind and rain, the path of the oncoming train and the iciness of the river water. In this hostile, threatening land Mark survives by attending very carefully and even fixedly on his environment. He sees not himself, not his frailty nor his fears for they make poor companions in such a land. Only his terror informs him and preserves him.

Understanding And Management Of Feelings

Children of alcoholics often experience feelings as the greatest threat, even more perilous than physical danger. Mark's history gives one explanation for this. Witnessing the physical abuse of one parent toward another or being the recipient of such abuse, has to provoke in a child many powerful feelings, including rage, shame, anxiety and terror. These are frightening feelings to have about one's parents. The parents are experienced as neither safe nor strong enough to be a sounding board for such emotion. These feelings provoke too much disloyalty for a child to reconcile with his coexisting love for and dependency on his parents.

Children at an early age are cognitively unable to distinguish between wishes and actions. Through interactions with their parents, children learn how to distinguish between feelings and behavior, how to express and manage feelings and how to control behavior. To be so enraged at a parent that one wishes the parent dead, may feel like the child has the power to kill the parent. That feeling is a terrifying one because the child is dependent on the parent. Parents who are reasonably comfortable with themselves and attentive to the needs and feelings of their children help children to express their anger while at the same time they set clear limits on what is acceptable behavior. Such parents can tolerate the child's rage, accept it without being overwhelmed or hurt by it and remain available and nonretaliatory towards the child. Through interactions with the parent the child learns over time and as development permits, how to manage such powerful feelings. When children feel that the parents are too dangerous (violent or retaliatory) or too vulnerable (to being narcissistically injured) they do not risk expressing such violent feelings and thus never learn the difference between feelings and actions. Instead those feelings are repressed or disowned because the child experiences them as potentially dangerous. If Mark's story is regarded as a metaphor and the danger of icy river and oncoming train represent the overwhelming feelings he may have toward his parents, then running away becomes the metaphor for how to cope with those feelings.

There are many ways to run away from feelings. Emotional pain can be expressed physically when there is no other outlet. Mark, as an adult, suffers chronically from pain. His therapist said of him, "He sees feelings in terms of pain." Based on psychological testing, it was found that he "avoids relating his feelings to their sources." This was noted by the people who treated Mark. They reported that each time he approached memories that evoked anger and the anger would start to emerge, Mark would suddenly become needy, demanding, actually childish in his demeanor. Then just as quickly he would repress all of this and his physical pain would recur. Hospital staff would notice that when Mark experienced physical pain, he became demanding and manipulative in attempts to get pain medication. He would whine and complain about staff inadequacy and insensitivity. When he was not in pain, he presented a very different picture, at those times seeing the staff as all helpful.

He also has externalized the problems, first by giving the internal pain (the emerging anger) a physical expression (his physical pain). He then transferred it to the nurses with whom he invested all the power for the relief of his pain through their giving or withholding of medication. Because he could not stay with his emotional pain, he could not take responsibility for coping with it. He therefore sees again all pain as coming from without when in fact in this instance the pain was internal, and a response to old memories. This can all be seen in Mark's story from age fifteen. The seeds of this pain were sown even earlier.

Externalization

Even in the "safe land" of the couple who befriended him, Mark focused outward and not toward the self. He attended to pleasing them without taking adequate notice of his own needs. In deciding that he must stay up all night so as not to be late for his first day's work he illustrates how fragile the sense of security even in this "sunny" land. In attempting to stay up all night Mark demonstrates that he may have been finely attuned to his environment, but he was poorly attuned to himself, to his capabilities and to his limitations. And so Mark, in focusing all his energy and attention onto his environment expends none on himself, none on understanding himself, appreciating his needs, recognizing both his strengths and his limitations.

These are important oversights and not uncommon to children of this land. They account for the ultimate lack of responsibility in people who perceive themselves as overly-responsible, but in fact are not. When people cannot recognize and, therefore, account for their limitations, they offer to do more than they can realistically do (such as Mark thinking he could stay up all night after his rigorous trip). This leads to unrealistic expectations and then disappointment and resentment on both sides of the interaction. Because there is no conscious awareness of what is causing the problems, all parties to such interactions are left confused and not understanding what is occurring.

In Mark's story it is important to note that he not only runs away from, he also runs toward a vision of a better life. In so doing though, he draws a picture of extremes, one a land of darkness and danger and the other of comfort and light. There is no light in the first and no dark in the second. Such a view gives Mark little room for negotiation or flexibility in either world. He either lives in abject misery or unconditional nurturing. This points to a brittleness in Mark's internal makeup that can prove counterproductive in the way he perceives his life. As he demonstrates in his interactions with the nurses regarding his medications, he experiences his environment as either all-depriving or all-giving and can see no middle ground, which allows him no room to negotiate with his either all-giving or all-depriving caregivers. This leaves him vulnerable to always feeling he is the victim, with deprivation and nurture always coming from without and always out of his own control. If he also treats his wife as the source of deprivation and control, this would account for at least some of their conflicts.

What we observe as Mark describes his world is someone who runs away to survive, turning his gaze sharply and narrowly outward in order to negotiate a perilous pathway. We see a person who has a very constricted ability to talk about feelings, to name, describe or even be aware of feelings. We perceive someone with an unrealistic sense of others' ability to take care of him, viewing the world in extremes of total nurturing or total deprivation. Finally we discern a person with little sense of his own inner workings or a realistic sense of his capabilities or limitations.

However we also see a man who has a keen sense of having survived that peril and who attributes his survival to some of the very qualities the clinician may define as self-limiting and counterproductive. We perceive someone who experiences existence very basically in terms of life and death and who experiences safety and nurturing as coming from outside the home. The phenomenon of being adequately taken care of is surrounded in Mark's mind by a dreamlike quality, as something not coming naturally to him but something he has to "run away toward". He cannot count on or trust that he will be cared for. The benevolence of parents is replaced by the "kindness of strangers" and to achieve this one has to attend to the "strangers," the outer life, the life away from the home and, by extension, the life away from the self. It is important for clinicians working with adult children of alcoholics to respect the power of the survival mechanisms and their importance. It is equally important for the users of those survival techniques to recognize that their use in adulthood is not as helpful as it was in childhood. Running away from feelings and externalizing all discomfort and all nurture compromises the quality of survival if one is attempting to lead a healthier and more satisfying life.

Avoidance

Like Mark, Billy ran away to survive. The third of four children, Billy grew up with a mother who used alcohol and a variety of prescription drugs to help her cope with a life that seemed overwhelming. Billy's father would ignore the drinking and drug taking for days and sometimes weeks by working late at the office or locking himself in his den to work or listen to music. Periodically he would complain to his wife about her drinking. Then, inevitably, there would be an argument. Depending on the stage of her inebriation, Billy's mother would either whimper quietly and then fall silent or respond loudly and even violently to her husband's complaints. She might scream at him, throw things or slam doors. Sometimes she'd grab a bottle of her tranquilizers and threaten to kill herself by swallowing the entire bottle. Sometimes she'd seize the keys to the car and go tearing off into the night. These scenes were terrifying to Billy. He feared for his mother's life whether by car accident or suicide. At such times he felt utterly helpless to ensure her safety or to protect himself from losing her.

When he was very young he tried to stop the arguments by physically coming between his warring parents. He soon learned this did not stop them and so he would retreat to his room. Eventually fatigue would overcome him and he would fall asleep. The next morning when he went downstairs, all signs of the struggle of the night before were cleared away. There was no broken glass and the car keys lay inanimate on the table, devoid of their lethal potency in the calm of the morning. His mother, with face drawn and pale from her sleepless, turbulent night of drinking, was otherwise unharmed. Billy soon learned that to climb into bed and pull the blankets about him to muffle the sounds of conflict, pain and violence was the best way to survive those ordeals.

"It worked," he said blandly, as he recalled those old scenes. This became a model for how he survived other unpleasant experiences. Billy not only learned to muffle distressing sounds coming from his environment but also distress coming from within himself. His mother was unavailable during the scary night and in the dreary morning after to encourage Billy to express his feelings about the night's events. In fact, she looked so fragile and uncomfortable the next morning, he dared not say anything to upset her for fear she would reach for the bottle of pills or alcohol again. With nowhere to express such strong feelings Billy learned to "muffle" them just as he had muffled the sounds coming from his arguing parents. He learned to avoid situations that would evoke strong feelings. When avoidance failed, he managed to suppress, repress and deny powerful feelings. Many adult children of alcoholics describe this blunting of their feelings. Said one young woman as she described what happens when she finds herself in a situation likely to generate strong emotion, "I numb out." A man described the same experience by saying, "When I think I'm going to get upset, I ice over."

Billy turned his energy into "making things right" in the family, keeping the peace when he could and reestablishing the calm after outbreaks. He became the apologist for his mother with his father by explaining, excusing her and covering up for her. He did this very quietly by always keeping a low profile and never calling attention to himself. He did well in school "to keep the peace," not because he cared about school. He was too preoccupied with the problems at home to attend very carefully to his own academic career. His native intelligence allowed him to do well despite his preoccupations. These preoccupations always were with the family and never with himself. He learned early to "pull the covers" over himself, over his own feelings, over his seeing anything he did not want to see or his hearing anything he did not want to hear.

His appearance as adult reflected this relinquishing of strong feeling. Tall, thin and handsome there was a blandness, an innocuous quality to his presentation. Soft-spoken, gentle and pleasant, there was rarely much inflection in his rather colorless speech. His eyes were very blue and very large but often stared vacantly ahead.

Always offering help to those around him, he was well liked by friends and colleagues and was never controversial or challenging. One can imagine him as a child: "loved" by his parents not for himself but for how easy he was to raise, how few demands he made on them and how much he did to allow them to be proud of him without their having to do much at all to take care of him. His handsomeness of appearance, his gentleness of manner and his lack of troublemaking must have led them to reinforce all the "choices" he made as to how to handle himself, his feelings, his way of "looking out" rather than "looking in" to survive. Billy runs away from feelings to survive, from his feelings, from the feelings of others and from any hint of pain, conflict or trouble.

Billy married a woman who, like his mother, also used pills and alcohol to cope. He had managed to keep this hidden from himself by only noticing how charming and loving she was when she wasn't drinking or overmedicating herself. So intent was he on keeping the peace that he overlooked how neglectful she had become of herself and the family. He shut out her constant complaining about him and how inattentive she felt he was towards her. Had he been more aware of his own displeasure at the way their relationship had deteriorated he might have also noticed how poorly she was doing. She began to make thinly veiled suicide threats, which he also muffled.

In the house, Billy kept a gun collection that he had inherited from his father. One night his wife, drunk and tearful, grabbed one of the guns. Claiming that Billy didn't care if she lived or died, she put the gun to her temple and pulled the trigger. Miraculously, the gun did not fire. "I went numb," Billy said flatly and matter-of-factly. "Then I took the gun from her, went upstairs and went to bed." He paused and then added, "I got through it, though." And even then Billy did not take the situation as seriously as it warranted and thus did not recognize that his wife needed treatment. Several weeks later when she brandished the same gun (he had not removed it from the house or even hidden it from her) and voiced the same suicidal threats at a party, their friends confronted Billy and helped him get her into a hospital that same night.

Billy's "adaptation" to living with the ongoing and frequently terrifying crises of childhood was to muffle or obliterate all signs of impending trouble because he was powerless to prevent the trouble. This adaptation in adulthood causes trouble. Billy blinds himself to both the external and internal experiences, to the behavior of his wife, which was clearly problematic; to the effects of her behavior on the marriage, which was also clearly a sign of trouble and to his feelings about her actions, feelings which also could have alerted him to the impending problems. Had he let himself be more aware of his wife's distress or the distress it was causing him and had he been more aware of the anger he was feeling in this situation, he might have been able to prevent a near suicide by helping his wife get help sooner and by not keeping guns in the house while she was vulnerable. Despite being directly confronted about this, he repeatedly insisted that having guns in the house with a potentially suicidal wife was not a problem.

This is an indication that something unconscious, something beyond the rational and objective is operating. Although Billy strongly insisted that he loved his wife and would do anything he could to keep her safe and get her help, his behavior did not support what he adamantly avowed. In fact, keeping the guns in the house actually threatened his wife's safety. Thus, the very adaptations that were to minimize or at least make the troubles bearable in his past added to those troubles in his adulthood. Billy never questioned them because they had originally helped him to survive.

Isolation Of Feeling

Emma's Story

Emma has no stories to tell about her childhood. Her past seems inaccessible to her. She has almost no memory. Her daughter Jackie, who also was alcoholic had told me that both Emma's father and ex-husband were alcoholics. Therefore, it was surprising to find out that Emma was not at all sure about the alcoholism of either of them. Her daughter at age twenty-two was now in inpatient treatment for a five-year alcohol and drug addiction. Emma had been unaware of her addiction.

I was also surprised at how Emma presented herself. Jackie while pretty is loud, labile, tough-looking, heavily made up and older looking than her years. In contrast, Emma, who was in her mid-forties, could have been mistaken for Jackie's sister. It was hard to believe that this very quiet, composed, delicate-looking woman was Jackie's mother. As opposed to Jackie who was outgoing and seemingly self-assured, Emma looked withdrawn and even frightened. She was dressed in a very prim business suit and sat rigidly and uncomfortably in the comfortable chair that I offered her.

When we began to talk about her professional life, her manner eased a little and she became more animated. It became clear as she described what she did that she was a successful business woman. When we talked about Jackie's complicated financial situation and living arrangements, Emma had a good grasp of the situation and what needed to be done to straighten out the chaos Jackie had created before entering the hospital. Emma was very clear about wanting to be a good parent for Jackie and very matter-of-fact, competent and knowledgeable about how she could help Jackie in these areas.

Then I tried to get some information about her past and about her daughter's early years. Again Emma tensed. Now as she spoke her voice became flat and devoid of all expression. She had little memory of her childhood or her marriage. Her speech was so unclear, vague and confused that it was hard to understand her.

When she could not remember, her eyes would look startled, as if to say, "I know I should be remembering these things and I'm not," but she did not remark on this. The clarity and competence of the early part of the interview was gone and I was left with the impression that Emma was a rather intellectually limited and unemotional woman with no propensity for reflection or introspection.

In our second session she began by quoting several modern philosophers. Although her discussion was disjointed and hard to follow, her intellectual grasp of the material was evident. However, her vagueness confused me. And then, as she was describing the philosophy that had so "profoundly" affected her life, she became strikingly clear: "Once I know I can end my life, it becomes easier not to." And then, her voice still a monotone, she described in detail suicidal impulses she had had since childhood. She slit her wrists as an adolescent. No one ever talked to her about it. Her parents took her to an emergency room for medical treatment but never discussed the incident with her. She was offered no help. She was asked no questions. She did not offer me this information, I had to ask questions to get it.

In the same monotone she also said that she had struggled with such impulses on and off throughout her life. Recently they had been strong again, but she told herself that because Jackie needed her, she knew she could not succumb to such urges. When I asked her what she did to control these impulses, she said that she would work very long hours and would involve herself in an extremely vigorous physical exercise program. As she talked, tears intermittently streamed down her cheeks. She seemed completely unaware of them. If I made any kind of empathic or comforting remark, she would quickly smile, shake her head and say, "But I'm happy. My life is fine. I'm okay." She seemed quite unaware of her emotions. When I asked her about her feelings she said that one of the few things she could remember about her childhood was a childhood fantasy. "I wanted to be like ice. Above everything. Untouched." Being like ice or being untouched was another form of running away from feelings and her emotional life. Emma's flight had been so radical that she had lost all touch with her inner life, except for her intellect. She had lost most of her memories; she had no awareness as tears rolled down her cheeks that she was anything but "happy." Sparing herself conscious pain, she continues to think about suicide and the tears continue to fall.

Like Billy, her adaptations often bring results opposite of what she would like. This again is our clue to the operation of unconscious processes. She managed to avoid the realization that her spouse was alcoholic and that he was being unfaithful to her. Although those realizations would have undoubtedly caused her pain, her avoidance of them caused even more: it kept her in a marriage for seventeen years that offered her little but unhappiness. Jackie has reported that her father was physically and sexually abusive to her, touching her inappropriately and playing so "rough" with her that on several occasions she had broken bones as a result of their "play." This too Emma avoided recognizing. She vaguely remembers Jackie's injuries but not their source. At moments she seems frightened by her lack of memory. The avoidance she has used to spare herself pain has prevented her from recognizing abuse to herself and her daughter. Recognition would have enabled her to take preventive measures. Her defenses prevent her from taking a responsible position in regard to her daughter and herself despite her obvious desire to be a responsible mother and human being and in direct contradiction of her image of herself as a concerned and responsive parent. In this case running from the pain creates more pain than facing the problem. In addition, her lack of awareness of her own feeling states has prevented her from getting help for the long-standing suicidal feelings that have significantly affected the quality of her life. Yet, Emma clings to her "adaptations" because unconsciously she links them with her survival.

Projection

There is yet another way to run away as Danny illustrates. Danny is the young emergency room resident who has been taking care of his alcoholic parents ever since he was a little boy. Danny uses projection. Projection is another defense mechanism. It is an unconscious process that enables a person to remain unaware of his unacceptable feelings by attributing them to someone else. On hearing a group of people who had alcoholic parents talk about their childhood Danny listened, engrossed, his eyes filling with tears periodically, a look of deep sadness on his face. Later while discussing the experience, he showed no awareness of his own reactions. Instead he spoke of the way the discussion seemed to be affecting someone else in the group, who in fact did not seem particularly moved by the discussion. Danny described the other's expression very much the way I might have described his own, but when I asked him how he felt, he looked puzzled and then continued to describe the reactions of others. Danny could not acknowledge such painful feelings and instead attributed them to others.

Crisis As Defense

Danny also runs in another way. He gravitates toward difficulty or crisis. Remember, that as a child he would be the one to decide when his parents needed medical treatment for alcohol-related injuries. He would gather his brothers together before making a decision, but the decision was always his. Danny as an adult has chosen to work in a hospital, repeating the medical decision making of his childhood. Working in the hospital emergency room ensures that he is always living on the edge of disaster, either his own or someone else's. When there is a crisis or threat of conflict, Danny intercedes. He takes over, he takes control. He will throw himself into problematic situations and become so caught up in them that he inappropriately gives orders to his superiors, just as he gave orders to his ailing parents as a child. Danny runs headlong *into* rather than *away from* crisis.

This also allows Danny to run away, by becoming so involved in other people's crises that he never has to look inward, to self-observe or to feel feelings that are directly related to himself. Some children of alcoholism describe the response to crisis as being like getting high. It charges the adrenalin, giving a sense of being needed, important and alive. This response also serves the same purpose as getting intoxicated by mobilizing feelings in a way that seems safe because those feelings are not really connected to the self. Other children of alcoholism complain that life is "boring" when their addicted spouse becomes sober and they are no longer caught up in the chaos of the addiction. Boring may be more accurately described as the gnawing discomfort when life is peaceful and one can no longer be distracted from turning inward by the crises of others.

Behaving Feelings

Alex's Story

Alex also uses a combination of defenses to run away from anyone or anything that causes him pain. One, the acting out of feelings rather than expressing them, proved tragic and near-fatal for him. To understand Alex, one must understand Alex's background.

Now at twenty-one, he cannot remember when his father did not drink. And for Alex, his father's drinking affected every aspect of his life. Drinking for Alex's father meant that his anger, which was always apparent, would increase and often erupt into violence. Like Alex his father also was the child of an alcoholic who began to drink alcoholically in early adulthood. A giant of a man, Alex's father stood 6'6" tall and was powerfully built. Even after several years of abstinence, his father bristled with a rage barely contained, spilling out in sarcasm, biting humor and rough "play." This rage was not contained at all when he drank.

Alex recalls that the extent of his father's violence seemed to be directly related to the amount of drinking he did. Alex reports that he could measure this by the time his father arrived home in the evening. So Alex would watch the clock. If his father came home at 6:30 p.m., this meant that he had stopped at a bar near work and just had a few drinks. He might then *look* normal, be merely irritable for the evening. Alex would still have to be on guard, careful not to do anything that might provoke his father. If his father did not arrive home until 8:00 p.m. then Alex could *see* that he had been drinking. He would walk a little differently; the expression on his face changed; his speech was slightly slurred. On these nights there would be angry exchanges with Alex's mother. These scenes left Alex tense and anxious. He would escape to his room to be out of his parents' way, but was unable to escape the sounds of their arguing. Unable to concentrate on homework or TV and unable to sleep, he lay in bed, staring at the ceiling, sisters across the hall, parents nearby, utterly alone.

It was even worse if his father came home later. Then, Alex could be quite sure, physical violence would follow his arrival. At various times his father had overturned furniture, put his fist through walls, emptied out the contents of a desk or thrown chairs through windows. He had also pushed Alex's mother around, slapping her and even punching her. When he was five or six years old, Alex had tried to break up these scenes by standing between his parents, protecting his mother and taking on his father. He quickly learned how futile were these attempts to intervene.

Alex's mother presented a very different picture. A study in contrasts, she was a large, attractive, solid-looking woman who often assumed the posture of a helpless little girl. A competent, no-nonsense business woman by day, she could be sometimes warm, flirtatious, and even seductive at home. But more often she seemed overwhelmed by her life in the family, reduced to the role of a submissive, passive victim. At times the strength and solidity she conveyed seemed inadequate to cover a frailty, a childlike fragility that emerged in relation to her husband. Alex's memories of his mother were colored by her vulnerability in the face of his father's violence.

These then were Alex's parents: an overpowering, frequently violent father and a mother whose strength and ability to survive were bound together with her helplessness, seductiveness and fragility. These models must have been confusing to Alex. Where was he to turn to be attended to and taken care of; who could soothe his fears, comfort him, reassure him and listen to him?

When his father was not drinking, he took an interest in Alex and did his best to look after him. He would play ball with him and help him with his homework. Even then Alex often could feel his father's anger lurking just beneath the surface. Alex assumed it was displeasure with him. He'd be sarcastic, play a little too roughly or walk off impatiently if Alex didn't catch on quickly enough to his explanation of a math problem. To Alex his father, even at the best of times, was always a threatening, hostile and unpredictable figure.

By contrast, Alex's mother could often be loving and affectionate when she was not in crisis. She was proud of Alex and seemed to enjoy his company, maybe even looking to Alex for comfort. But frequently Alex's mother *was* in crisis. At those times she became preoccupied and unable to attend to Alex's needs. She implored him never to become an alcoholic like his father. Rather than worry about himself, Alex began to worry about her. He felt more the need to protect her than be protected by her. Because he did not want to add to her burden he did not complain to her, he did not tell her how frightened and angry he was nor ask her for help with his own increasingly difficult life. Over and over he promised her that he would never become like his father.

Yet at fifteen Alex began to drink. By seventeen he had wrecked a car and suffered a concussion. His drinking continued to get worse. The denial flourished, reinforced by early experiences and by his determination never to be like his father. "I was never a mean drunk, always a happy drunk," he insisted. His mother's denial matched his own as she concurred with this. The denial, unconfronted anywhere, allowed his drinking to get worse. He had another serious car accident. At eighteen he began working at high risk jobs, including construction work on high steel beams. The more dangerous the work, the more he seemed to relish it. He ignored the seriousness of yet another car accident and continued to drink and drive. At age nineteen he had one more accident. This one he could not ignore. It left him crippled for life, paralyzed forever from the waist down.

Alex spent the better part of a year hospitalized for the treatment of his injuries. He never touched his feelings about his loss, nor did he face his alcoholism. Despite his knowledge that his drinking had robbed him forever of the use of half his body, Alex left the hospital and went home to continue to drink. Once again, his drinking grew worse. His risk-taking also persisted, now confined to poor self-care of his body and dangerous use of his wheelchair. Both had the potential for being life-threatening.

Alex was twenty-one when he entered inpatient treatment for his alcoholism. He presented himself as a handsome, strapping young man, confined for life to a wheelchair. He quickly endeared himself to the community with his gentle, appealing manner. Despite his own limitations he reached out to others he perceived as vulnerable or in need of help. Like his mother, he was a study in contrasts: great power and helplessness, strength and weakness. The muscles in his arms, shoulders and chest bulged. The massive strength in his upper body contrasted sharply with the shriveled legs resting inert and useless on the wheelchair footrest. As if in defiance and denial of his disability, his actions in the wheelchair were daredevil, reckless and wild. He would careen down long hospital ramps, stopping just inches away from person or object. With only his arms and torso to support him, he would lower himself and his chair down steep flights of steps, leaving others gasping and helpless as they watched, expecting him to lose his balance or strength and go crashing down the stairs.

But those he considered vulnerable or in need of his care would never see this wild side. He always remained protective, considerate and helpful. No matter what posture Alex assumed, his eyes seemed always to have a life of their own — large and gentle and sad.

Both Alex's wildness and his gentleness have their roots in the same soil where his alcoholism grew. They are nourished by the same inner springs, which, if not properly channeled, might destroy him. Already paralyzed, unable to walk or run, he has not been slowed down by his tragedy. He has not faced what is crippling him, possibly because not facing feelings is what originally allowed him to survive.

Both Alex's risk taking and his caretaking may be expressions of the same inner turmoil that Alex is unable to face. From watching both his father and his mother, Alex learned coping strategies that have become embedded in his character, shaping his style of responding to people and situations. He never questions them because they have become inextricably bound to his survival. Above all, he learned that expression of feelings can be deadly. Expressing anger destroys objects and hurts people. Feelings lead inevitably to arguments and violence. Expression of feelings threatens a little boy's survival. Therefore one must suppress, repress and deny feeling. Alex avoids his emotion by acting on it rather than by feeling it, by drinking, by daredevil acts, by hurting himself. The hideous irony is that by running away from his feelings, Alex has destroyed his ability to run, has irrevocably crippled himself forever.

CHAPTER 6

Memory Compromised:
The Loss Of One's Past

. . . What sort of a life (if any), what sort of a world, what sort of a self, can be preserved in a man who has lost the greater part of his memory and, with this, his past, and his moorings in time?

Oliver Sacks

This question, posed by neurologist Oliver Sacks in his book *The Man Who Mistook his Wife For A Hat,* begins a discussion of the profound effects of the loss of memory due to organic impairment. Dr. Sacks also quotes Luis Buñuel on the devastation that occurs when a person loses most of his memory: "Our memory is our coherence, our reason, our feeling, even our action." Both men, scientist and artist, physician and filmmaker, point to the influence of memory on a person's thoughts, feelings, behavior and even self-image. In each case they are discussing the ravages of age or disease on memory that was initially intact. Is the impact any less devastating when the initial impressions of the experiences that become memory are so compromised by denial and other distortions that memory itself has little integrity? What then can be said of memory's influence on "our coherence, our reason, our feeling, even our action?" A childhood of alcoholism ravages memory in several different ways.

The Absence Of Memory

In the last chapter, running away was described as the paradigm for various ways to cope. People run away from conflict, from pain and from distress. They even run away from memory when the past is too painful to remember. Incidents, people, even whole years or periods in a life may be lost when memory is sealed off as a form of self-protection.

Carrie's Story

Carrie lives with dramatic gaps in her memory. She can spellbind an audience with vivid stories about her rebellious childhood and adolescence, but has no memories of her father during that very same period in her life. Carrie, now in her mid-fifties, is overweight, careless about her appearance, unattractively dressed but with a face that must have been very pretty before time and drink exacted their toll. She has survived three marriages and a near devastating course of alcoholism. Her father, too, was alcoholic.

"He left home on my ninth birthday," she reports, her voice devoid of all inflection as she speaks. "It was during my birthday party. He came home drunk and told my mother to get all the kids out of the house. My mother said, 'No, you get out.' And he did," Carrie continues, her voice flat. She pauses, staring blankly ahead, and then adds, "He never came back. My mother used to tell me it was my fault that he left, because it happened at my birthday party." Carrie's face and her voice continue to be without expression as she speaks. She shows no reaction either to the loss of her father or to the attribution of blame by her mother.

When I ask her what her father was like, Carrie remarks that she has no memory of him, no memory at all. For the first time her voice takes on life as she continues, finally looking at me, engaging me for the first time in her story.

> I can remember the dresses I wore each Easter as a child, but I can't remember my father. I can remember the house where we lived. I remember his room, his dresser, the brush and comb that sat on top of it. I remember his closet and his bed; I even remember the linens on the bed. But I don't remember my father.

As she shifts position in her chair, her eyes roam the room as if searching for something. Her gaze returns to me again, "I look at pictures with him in them and I have no memory of the events they're recording."

After he left, for a while he would come back to visit. Carrie
. remembers a time when he took Carrie and all her siblings on an
outing, but again she cannot remember her father. He took them to
a farm that belonged to a friend.

> I remember my father's friend. I remember the farm. I remember
> sitting around this big table having lunch. We had hoagies. I know
> my father was at that table. I see everyone else. I even see the
> hoagies. But I can't see my father.

The intensity with which Carrie looks at me as she tells this part of
the story is not one of opening up but rather of keeping shut. There
is no curiosity in her words or expression. She seems to be warning
me not to ask questions and not to open doors she has purposely
kept shut for so long. There seems a pride, or perhaps defiance, in
her demeanor as she describes the totality of her memory block.
Only once was there a wavering in this position; that was when she
rather shyly asked if this was abnormal, to have her father so radically
sealed off from her recall. But the question had to do with her
normality, not the desire to retrieve the lost memories.

Carrie's lack of ambivalence about her inability to remember her
father indicates that this could be a self-protective measure with
several possible intentions. It may spare her awareness, both then
and now, of the pain and rage at the sudden and irrational loss of
her father, a loss that must have been very difficult for her to
comprehend or accept. Considering that her mother told her it was
her fault that her father left, it is clear her mother was unable to help
her deal with the loss. Her lack of memory may also help spare her
the guilt caused by her mother's accusation. She may have also felt
rage at her mother for sending her father away and then blaming her
for it. This rage may have been too threatening to experience.

Remember Buñuel's linkage of memory with coherence, feeling,
reason and action. Carrie seems deficient in all of these areas. She
is as cut off from feeling and self-understanding as she is from
memories of her father and the meaning of his behavior and its
effect on the family. Carrie did not say, as do many children of
alcoholism, that she hated her father's drinking, even though it had
dire consequences on her life. Although the lack of memory is not
necessarily the reason for her being this cut off from herself, it is
certainly congruent with it. If she instinctively cuts off memory in
the same way she blocks off other inner processes, such as feeling,
she closes off all avenues toward awareness of the self. Memory

could stimulate feelings, help her attach meanings to her behavior and his if she let it. She does not.

Nor does Carrie seem to think about her father's drinking or her mother's equally destructive behavior. She seems just as nonreflective about the consequences of her own alcoholism and other self-destructive behavior on her life. Although there can be many reasons for this, her absence of memory helps reinforce her denial. Equally significant, this absence may have robbed her of the ability to attach meaning to the alcoholism and the ensuing events that surrounded it. By not remembering this most important part of her life, she is prevented from thinking about it and its effects on her. Carrie's keen intelligence, as reflected by her sharp wit and high I.Q. score is not manifested in her ability to reflect about her life, to give it meaning and to see the past as influencing the present or the present as repeating patterns from the past. She does not connect events with feelings or motivations or reasons. It is as if she floats disconnectedly through her life, not seeing patterns or themes, not connecting past experience with current behavior, as if she has lost her "moorings in time."

Pat's Story

Pat did not think Carrie's story unusual because hers was so similar. Instead of floating disconnectedly, Pat seems more cut off from her past. When she looks back she stares directly at a blank wall, an image she uses to describe her lack of memory. She knows her father was alcoholic because her sisters told her he was. He died when she was eight years old. She could not remember anything about him, not even what he looked like. She does remember the day of his death. She remembers a nun at school calling her into her office and telling her that she had to go home. She remembers that she knew something was wrong but there was no memory of any feeling attached to that knowledge. When she was told that her father had died, she remembers wondering what she was supposed to do and how she was supposed to react. That is the only memory she has of her father's death. According to Pat no one in the family ever talked about him after his death. Thus, the shutting off of memory was complete and never challenged. When asked what it was like to have no memories of her father she shrugged and then replied, "How can you miss something if you never had it?"

Neither Pat nor Carrie show any visible discomfort with the lack of memory of their fathers. Pat elaborates on her attempts to remember him, "It's like being in front of a brick wall." When I asked if it bothers her, she laughs, "Hell, I spent years building it!" There is no anxiety visible as she talks. The way each of these women deal with their memories is similar to how they each deal with their feelings. They seal them off and run away from them.

Carrie either acts out her feelings through her behavior or she somatizes, meaning that she expresses them through physical symptoms. She never describes feelings when she talks about parts of her past that she does remember. She talks instead about getting drunk, getting thrown out of college and getting divorced. When asked how she feels, she always responds with a description of her physical well-being. Each time she faces emotional stress she gets a cold or a stomachache or some other physical ailment. Then, instead of examining the emotional pain, she describes the physical symptom. Initially this was adaptive because she learned early that it was not safe to express emotions. Unexpressed feelings will always find some outlet when no direct relief is available. Thus, the body may react to the internal pressure by getting sick. However, such a position does not remain adaptive. The focus on the physical prevents her from understanding the psychological, the way her feelings are influencing her behavior and even her thinking. This focus also prevents her from taking control of her life, so alienated is she from the feelings that drive her behavior. Her memories could help her to build a fuller sense of herself. Without them she seems condemned to act out rather than act on her life.

Pat has alienated herself from her feelings, erecting a "brick wall" to defend not only against memory, but also against any strong feelings or perceptions that might cause her conflict. She recognizes that this is a problem. She also realizes that the brick walls she creates prevent her from learning from her mistakes and keep her repeating old patterns and behaviors that consciously she does not want to recreate. And while she says that she is not bothered by her lack of memory, she keeps returning to it and keeps talking about it, as if curling around the edges of the blackness she has imposed, is a thread of light she would like to uncover.

Denial

Rick's Story

Rick illustrates the impact of his family's denial on his memory. He was forty-two years old when he entered treatment for a poly-drug addiction. Although he had achieved a significant amount of success in his professional life, he had failed at two marriages and found his relationship with his three children strained and difficult. Articulate, sharp-witted and often charming he could also be manipulative, dishonest, intimidating and distancing with his anger, his verbal attacks and his complaints. He had been in therapy for many years.

Rick, despite his preoccupation with his past and particularly with his difficult and even cruel mother, had no idea that she was a substance abuser. She had used pills to treat a myriad of ailments and had also given them to Rick from the time he was very young. She also "drank a little." When Rick finally entered inpatient treatment for his own chemical dependency, a counselor who took his drug and alcohol history suggested to him that his mother sounded like she too was chemically dependent. Rick thought his counselor was "crazy" but agreed to come to the adult children of alcoholics group being offered to inpatients to explore the matter more thoroughly.

The group opened that day with two members talking about the violence they had experienced at the hands of their alcoholic parents. Describing breakfast, one man related, "The eggs would be sliding down the wall if he (his alcoholic father) didn't like the way my mother prepared them." A middle-aged woman then related tearfully a scene where her father chased her around the house with a golf club.

At first Rick seemed uncomfortable with the process and interrupted several times as emotion grew intense around a painful memory. Gradually he settled down and became increasingly engaged in the discussion. He watched each person as they spoke, hanging on their every word. Finally, sitting on the edge of his chair, his voice somewhat hushed with almost a note of awe, he sighed, "This is the most overwhelming group I have ever been in . . ." He then went on to explain that as he listened to the stories he realized his tremendously conflictual and often traumatic experiences with his mother, experiences he felt had shaped his life in profound ways, were related to her addiction. He had not recognized this until the stories began to unsettle him.

"When I first came into the group I wanted to say, 'I don't belong here; there were no eggs on the wall.' You know, there *were* eggs on the wall. She threw oranges at me. She scratched my face. She kept me grounded for an entire month for nothing. My life was totally dependent on her moods and I never knew what they would be. I developed a pattern to my life, based on my relationship with her and to avoid her wrath: lying, exaggerating, sliding this way and that, never confronting a situation and using drugs to cope." He looked down, inward, shaking his head, "Never once did I think she was addicted until today."

Redefined in the light of this new information, memories returned. He remembered her ordering pills in enormous quantities from the pharmaceutical companies (ostensibly for his father who was a doctor). He knew the names of all her pills and the reason she took each one. He remembered her giving him amphetamines to "perk me up" and other pills to "relax me when I couldn't sleep." But he never connected her unpredictable, abusive behavior with her drug use. Almost to himself he mumbled, "Did my father know? Was he overprescribing for himself, too?" Once some old perceptions are redefined, it is as if all things are now called into question and all memory is challenged.

Thinking aloud he continued, "This changes things for me. I grew up disliking my mother. I took pleasure in calling her a bitch, in saying she was rotten and no good. Now that I learn she had an addiction, can I still say that about her? Does this change how I'm supposed to feel about her? This is very confusing." Throughout the rest of that group session, Rick alternated between confusion and a dawning understanding.

Clearly, a new way of understanding his past does not change that past nor the effects it had on him; but breaking through the denial and the distortions of memory resulting from that denial could significantly affect Rick. No newcomer to therapy, he has been over his past before but always with the distortions of the denial to color his memory. Perhaps removing that distortion will provide him with clearer perceptions and will help to reshape memory so that it can be more useful and coherent to him. Recognizing his mother was chemically dependent may ultimately lead him to thinking differently about himself, about his feelings and reactions to her and about his own, until now intractable addiction. It could help him redefine old issues that he has worked on previously in therapy without resolution. Coming face to face with another aspect of his past could provide him with an impetus to move past the impasse he's been struggling with in therapy for so many years.

Memory Compromised

Carl's memory was intact, vivid even. However, remembering lead only to a perceived confusion because the memories were colored by his parents' denial. Carl remembers a life of inconsistency that went from a drab and sometimes nightmarish life at home to an idealized, dreamlike life on the family's yacht. He distinctly remembers seeing his father passed out on the living room sofa, thinking he was dead and being told gruffly by his mother that his father was only asleep. Carl remembers feeling confused because what his mother told him in no way validated what he was perceiving. Carl looks painfully confused as he talks about these memories.

It is obvious to those who hear Carl's story that his father was alcoholic, a binge drinker who drank alcoholically each time he drank, even if the drinking did not occur every day, every week or even every month. It is clear to an informed observer that the drinking was alcoholic and explained much of what Carl experiences as inexplicable. It is obvious to everyone but Carl, that is.

Until Carl came into treatment for his own alcoholism at age thirty-four, he had no idea his father was alcoholic. Even after it was explained to him, he could not think of his father in those terms, perhaps because he never had. Explanation at this late date has not decreased Carl's all-pervasive confusion as it relates to his past. Although Carl's memory is intact, it only serves to sustain and maintain his confusion rather than to inform, clarify and attach meaning to important events of his life.

Memory In Support Of Denial

Rick's memory was compromised by his parents' denial. Ruth's memory is affected by her own denial. She is the woman who reported with such warmth how she loved her mother's homemade bread. Her memories of her childhood were filled with scenes of verbal and physical abuse from her alcoholic, sadistic father. He pushed and slapped her, made fun of her and criticized her. Those memories bring tears, making her shudder with repulsion as they flood her with feelings she is unused to experiencing.

Ruth's whole countenance changes when she talks about her mother's homemade bread. But as she is asked to look at this memory more carefully and to put it in context, it unfolds that the pleasure she connects to this memory may be shielding her from a very unpleasant, perhaps unbearable realization: that perhaps her mother was not really taking such good care of her by providing her with this wonderful bread. This bread was used to allow Ruth's father to take the more substantive food for himself. Her father was served first "to keep the peace," and reportedly took all the meat. Her mother did nothing further to adequately provide for the children. The memory of bread provides a screen to deny the mother's inability to protect her children from their father's selfishnesss and cruelty. It may even provide an exaggeration of the father's behavior, devaluing him to the same possibly unrealistic extent that it idealizes the mother.

In the stories about the cruelty of her father, Ruth never mentioned her mother and her mother's inability to protect Ruth. While this use of memory to suppress any negative recollection of her mother may seem self-protective and may seem to help Ruth maintain a positive relationship with at least one parent, Ruth seems always brimming with a rage that does not abate, despite ongoing expressed anger at her father. I wonder if some of this anger is not meant for her mother, and will not abate until Ruth can look at the mix of feelings she must have about her mother. By protecting herself from awareness of her rage at her mother, she does not have the opportunity to examine that anger and eventually work it through.

The memory of the homemade bread seems to preserve for Ruth a tiny island of pleasantness in an otherwise bleak and hostile landscape. Although the memory itself may have been accurate, the bread may very well have been delicious and her mother warm and loving at times, this same memory serves to maintain an illusion for Ruth, an illusion of a mother more nurturing and caregiving than she may have actually been. Living with such an illusion has not helped Ruth come to terms with her anger.

Affective Memory

Becky can remember the events of her past, but she has no affective memory connected to these events. She insists "it wasn't really so bad" growing up with her alcoholic mother. It slips out that Christmas dinner was usually anywhere from one to four hours late. She knows those weren't the only late meals but those are the ones she remembers most vividly. She quickly repeats, "It wasn't that bad." Giggling nervously, she rushes on with her story. She describes her first date as an adolescent and the fact that her mother was drunk when she greeted the boy at the door. When I ask what that was like, Becky sucks in her breath and answers softly, "Oh, I don't know. I guess I was a little embarrassed. I don't really remember." She quickly changes the subject.

In changing the subject, Becky seems to be running away. It is unclear whether she is running away from the emotion threatening to flood her if she lets it emerge into consciousness, or whether she is running from her lack of feeling or memory of any feeling about the incident. Becky, an articulate young woman, is always examining herself and her behavior. She obsesses endlessly with words, with theories to explain her actions to herself, as well as her reactions and her interactions with the important people in her life. This would indicate an understanding that her quick change of subject belies. As she brushes against the old memories she sucks in her breath and quickly pulls back. Usually careful and thorough in exploring every thought and feeling, she runs away when it comes to a memory so tender, so fraught with feeling, that threatens to cause more pain than she may think she can endure.

Or is the phenomenon she is up against actually an absence of emotional memory? Did she so effectively repress the feelings experienced in childhood that in adulthood they are truly unavailable to her? Her quick change of subject then would be more connected to covering up the lack of emotion as she talked to me, sensing that somehow she should be remembering some feeling and covering up the fact that she was not. In either case, Becky does not have the emotion available to her to connect it to important, meaningful memories from her past. While that might seem a benefit to Becky, for it spares her the pain attached to those old memories, it is not in her best interest in the long run. While those feelings are not in Becky's conscious awareness, they are still within her and exert an influence on her life that she cannot control because of her lack of awareness. If she were able to recall and experience some of that old pain she might then also be able to let go of it and its influence on her present life.

Silence Stifles The Memory

Finally, even when memory survives intact, and even when the feeling is still attached to the memory, the silence that surrounds a child of alcoholism may cause that memory to haunt him.

Jim is a sixty-four year old retired clergyman who has been fighting a losing battle with his own alcoholism for 30 years. He is also the son of an alcoholic. He had never spoken to anyone about his father's alcoholism until he entered inpatient treatment for his own illness. There he was put into a therapy group for adult children of alcoholics. After listening for a short time to the discussion of what it was like growing up with an alcoholic parent, he softly interrupted and began to speak. He described a day when he was fourteen years old. His father, in a drunken rage, pushed him down a flight of stairs. Tears began to run down his cheeks as he spoke. He paused, still tearful, and shook his head, "I never spoke of this before," he said. He then fell silent, tears still running silently down his face. As others spoke, he seemed to half listen to them and half listen to his memories. When group members would periodically and very gently ask him how he was, he would simply shake his lowered head and softly repeat, "I never talked about this before." Toward the end of the group session, his tears subsiding, he looked up, eyes bright and hard and said, "You know, I still have nightmares about this. About being thrown down those stairs. I still dream about it frequently."

The memory of an incident that had occurred 50 years before had the immediacy and impact as if it had just occurred, held captive by the silence that surrounded it and encapsulated it. Rather than inform him, warn him, explain to him, the memory traps him in a past he would prefer to forget because of the silence that envelops it. The silence isolates him and keeps him from talking. The silence also prevents him from getting comfort and feedback from others. Placed in a proper context, the memory could have been used to work through some of his feelings about his father, his father's alcoholism and its effects on Jim. Instead, trapped by the silence, the memory continues to haunt him.

CHAPTER 7

Looking Away
Perception Compromised

Children who survive in a land where they do not feel safe or adequately protected by those who take care of them, learn to take care of themselves. Early in life children of alcoholism become vigilant, even hypervigilant, ever alert for physical or emotional danger, whether that danger be physical or sexual abuse or subjection to ridicule, embarrassment, cruel criticism or devaluation. Threats to a child's safety come from several sources: actual aggressive or hostile behavior on the part of the parents; a lack of protectiveness of the child and insufficient attention to the child's needs and well-being. In each case, these threats come from the environment surrounding the child. To meet those threats and to persevere, children develop a vision that is always turned outward, focused on the people and the events of their lives, for there lies the source of the problems they encounter. This keenly attuned alertness becomes a valuable asset because it enables them to become excellent predictors of crisis and to sense potential problems long before their less sensitized peers. They also become extremely sensitive to the moods, needs and especially the limitations and vulnerabilities of others, again because that is where their attention is focused.

However, there are also drawbacks to this kind of vision. Eventually, all sources of conflict and stress are seen as coming from external origins (from the people and the events around them) and never as internally derived or motivated (coming from within the self). In attending to the external children focus away from themselves. They not only run away from their internal life, but they also look away, failing to see uncomfortable feelings, thoughts or perceptions. In looking away, they further distance themselves from their inner lives, and from the sense of who they are. In looking away to save themselves, they lose themselves.

Mark, who ran away from home at age fifteen to escape a violently alcoholic home life, illustrates this. He describes a land that was perilous and fraught with danger and that can be seen as a metaphor for the physical and emotional abuse he was subjected to by his violently alcoholic father. Typically, he does not describe the feelings that led him to run away but instead the landscape itself, and that in great detail. In order to negotiate the perils of that land, he had to be ever alert to the environment, to the muddy fields, the icy river and the railroad tracks. In his entire description he used only one feeling word: terror, to describe his reaction to an oncoming train directly in his path. Focusing outward, the exquisite detail of his description is reserved only for the land and not for himself. To focus on his own feelings at such a time might have been counterproductive. His own fear might have paralyzed him; his desire to be cared for more adequately might have prevented him from taking care of himself.

Self-preservation in this situation depends on attending very attentively to potential threat coming from a hostile environment. Self-preservation also comes from looking just as carefully away from the self, *not* attending to one's feelings of fear, anxiety, helplessness or rage and even from ignoring one's hunger for attention and nurturing. Needs may not be sufficiently satisfied by others and feelings may have no adequate outlet. When that is the case, those needs and feelings then become part of the threat because they have no way of becoming part of the solution. When awareness of the inner life becomes a threat, then one is alienated from oneself, as if living with a stranger.

Focusing Away From Conflict

Because this perception is linked with survival, whether it be physical or psychological survival, then the way it is used will always be survival-oriented. To be effective as a survival mechanism, this vision is not only turned outward but also narrowly focused, selective and circumscribed to the area of threat over which one has control. These children turn away from conflict and emotional stress not only from within, but from the environment as well when they have no control over it. If children were to focus on threats to survival over which they had no control, then their anxiety would become intolerable. The adaptive response to such situations is to look only at that over which they have control, therefore eliminating overwhelming and nonproductive anxiety. One woman, as she was describing the endless fighting she used to witness nightly between her parents (and over which she soon found she had absolutely no control) told proudly of how she had learned to block it out. "I would be sitting between my two parents watching TV and they would start to argue. I'd be so intent on the program I'd never even hear them. They could scream at each other right across me and I'd just keep watching the set and never hear a thing."

I witnessed a nine-year-old boy perform such a feat in my office. During a family session with him, his younger sister and his two parents, he asked if he could have a coloring book. I gave him one, but it lay ignored in his lap for the early part of the interview as he listened most attentively and participated in the proceedings. When his parents touched on a conflictual issue, the tension between them suddenly escalated. Although this tension was not verbally expressed it was quite obvious nonetheless. When I asked him what he thought about his parents' discussion he was suddenly engrossed in the coloring book. When I repeated his name, he looked up startled and then said he had not heard anything that had been said. His sensibilities ever alert for the dreaded conflict (his parents were in fact considering divorce and hinting about it in front of the children but not openly discussing it), he quickly looked away as soon as it began, losing himself in the coloring book so as not to hear what he dared not hear.

This turning away from situations that are conflictual or inherently stressful when he felt he had no control over the outcome may have seemed adaptive to the little boy but in fact it is tremendously constricting. It reinforces the incorrect assumption that survival is the issue. It also reinforces the impression, that derives from the way he sees his parents deal with conflict, that conflict is dangerous and inevitably leads to the threat of separation and loss. This need not be the case, but the fears the assumption generates lead him to avoid facing conflict. His avoidance then deprives him of the opportunity to learn that working toward the resolution of interpersonal conflicts can be a process that promotes healthy growth, increased understanding of the other, increased flexibility in problem-solving skills and a better understanding of the value of compromise. To keep narrowly focused prevents him from seeing options that might have appeared if his vision were not so limited. While keeping his vision narrowly focused may help Mark negotiate a physically perilous land, it may not at all help this anxious nine-year-old boy negotiate his parents' possible divorce. Although he will never be able to control whether or not his parents divorce, he may be able to lessen his own anxiety and come to a more realistic appraisal of the threats to his own survival if they were to separate. To do this he has to be able to face the problem and to be open to seeing all the possibilities. This only can be accomplished by talking about them and by examining them, preferably with an older, wiser person. The dilemma for such children is unfortunately that there often is no other person with whom to talk and problem solve. This leads to nine-year-olds seeing no other option but to stop seeing.

Focusing On The Environment

Katie's Story

Katie illustrates the pressure to keep forever focused outward as a response to a hostile, depriving and non-nurturing environment. To attend to her own needs or feelings before those of her mother's could bring real trouble for Katie. One of two sisters of two alcoholic parents, it was their mother's alcoholism that was the most troublesome to the girls. Katie never knew when she came home from school each day what would await her. Sometimes her mother would be pleasantly awaiting the girls' arrival home with an after-school snack prepared for them. Her mother would be alert and interested to hear what had happened that day in school. On those afternoons Katie and her sister would snack, chat with their mother and then go out to play. They could be reasonably assured that when they returned home dinner would be ready, and there would be quiet time to do their homework during the evening, followed by an uninterrupted night's sleep.

On other afternoons it would be different. As Katie opened the front door and glanced in at the living room, she could tell by the state of disarray that her mother was drinking. If her mother were not already waiting for them, Katie and her sister would hurry to their room, quickly change into their play clothes and get out of the house as quickly as possible. There was no time to stop for a snack, whether they were hungry or not. The most important thing was to avoid contact at such times with their mother. If they were lucky on such afternoons, she would be nowhere in sight. On those days when Katie and her sister returned home after playing, they could never be sure whether there would be a dinner prepared for them. Sometimes it had been started and then forgotten, and was either lying scorched in the sink or dried out and burnt in the oven. At other times the kitchen was dark and empty; clearly the preparation of dinner was not even given a thought. In either case Katie knew that if they were to eat at all on such nights, she and her sister would have to sneak into the kitchen and find cold leftovers or make do with cookies and potato chips. Katie's blindness to her own needs is so complete that she insists as an adult that she prefers potato chips and cookies to a real dinner and frequently is content with that when her drug-addicted husband does not come home for dinner. This becomes more comfortable, perhaps more bearable than seeing the deprivations that accompany living with an addicted parent or spouse.

At such times in Katie's childhood there would be more missing than a hot dinner. On those nights, when Katie's father arrived home and found the house in disarray and dinner unprepared, he would fix himself a drink and then go searching for his wife. Inevitably an argument would ensue. Just how long the arguing would continue usually depended on how many drinks he fixed for himself. Sometimes it ended abruptly, unresolved, with each parent retreating in sullen silence, into separate rooms. On those evenings the house was full of a tense quiet. The girls listened anxiously to the silence, waiting for it to erupt into more arguing, which sometimes happened. Gone for the night was a peaceful quiet, the kind that would enable the girls to give careful attention to their homework. Instead attention was to the silence and what it covered. They would fall asleep on such nights tense and listening to the silence.

At least on those nights they slept, perhaps not peacefully, but at least without interruption. On other nights even their sleep was interrupted by the sporadic arguing, sometimes lasting well into the night. The arguing which often got loud, was sometimes punctuated by a banging door, by a fist slamming into a table or wall or by a piece of furniture being kicked or pushed into another object. Katie knew this was influenced by how much her father had had to drink. But she never knew whether it was because he stopped after one drink and did not let the sedative effects of the alcohol soothe him into a passive acceptance of his wife's drinking behavior or whether it was because he kept on drinking and let the alcohol loosen his inhibitions to complain more vocally and irritably than he did when not drinking.

There were other afternoons when Katie and her sister arrived home and their mother was waiting for them with a wild look in her eyes. She would scream at them that their room was a mess and that they were bad and irresponsible and that they were not to go out to play until their room had been straightened. In particular, she complained about their bureau drawers. They climbed the stairs heavily on such days, knowing what they would find as they entered their room. The bureau drawers were all standing wide open and empty, their clothes and other personal possessions strewn on the floor in front of the dresser. They carefully and quietly picked up the clothes and put them neatly back in the drawers. When their mother with drink in hand, came in to inspect, she would scream that they still were not neat and once again would dump the contents of the drawers onto the floor. On such days, Katie and her sister might spend the entire afternoon neatly filling the bureau drawers, while listening to their mother berating them and complaining about her ill fortune to have two such miserable daughters.

In attempts to avoid such scenes Katie would keep focused on her mother rather than herself. As Katie entered her home after school each day, she glanced quickly at the living room. Its condition, she had learned, would inform her as to the state of her mother's drinking. If Katie were to attend instead to how hungry or tired she was herself, she might miss the fact that her mother was drinking and would be looking for Katie so that she could criticize her or engage her in some meaningless task to keep her trapped and miserable in the house all afternoon. As a means of protecting herself from her mother's drunkenness, Katie's attention must be turned outward toward the condition of the house and her mother rather than toward herself. Far more important than whether or not she wanted something to eat or a chance to play quietly in her room after school, was whether her mother had started to drink. If she had started, Katie had to try to get out of the house as quickly as possible to avoid her. Katie eventually learned that her comfort and her ultimate well-being came from looking away from herself and toward others and her environment.

This hyperalertness to an alcoholic parent's condition is frequently reported. One man described being able to tell by the sounds of his father's car as he pulled into the driveway whether or not he had been drinking. Another spoke of being in bed at night and able to tell by his father's footsteps as he climbed the stairs whether he had been drinking. It was important for him to know, because when drunk his father had on several occasions punched the boy as he slept. Focusing on his father's footsteps became self-protective in an environment that did not protect him. Each time his father performed a violent act, he reinforced the belief that his son was not safe, that survival was a real issue, and that for his son to endure he had to attend not to his own feelings but instead to his father and the degree of his father's drunkenness.

As Katie told her story to me many years later, now an adult with children of her own, her face was ashen, her fists were clenched with nails digging into her palms; her voice was almost a whisper, flat and devoid of intonation or feeling. Her eyes stared vacantly ahead as if not wanting to see or remember what she was relating. When asked if she had talked about this before, she said only rarely. When asked to elaborate, she explained that, of course, she could never mention such scenes to her mother. If she were to confront her mother while she was drinking, it would only increase her mother's rage, which was already too frightening to Katie. If she were to bring it up the next day, when her mother was sober but sullen, Katie was afraid it might upset her mother and trigger another round of drinking. So there was no good time to tell her, even if she were to feel comfortable enough with her (which of course she did not). Being unable to talk to her mother kept Katie's anxiety unrelieved. It further deepened her perception that she was living with someone unpredictable and potentially destructive. Therefore, she must remain always on alert for the danger that persistently threatened to overpower her.

Nor was Katie able to find another safe person to help her with this terrible predicament. She had tried to tell her father once or twice when she was still very young. The first time he was startled, paused and then shrugged with a smile, "Oh come now, Katie, it can't be that bad. You must be exaggerating." There was something about the way he responded that made Katie feel ashamed, as if she had said something wrong that she should not have said. He seemed to be implying that she was making it up and even though she knew she was not, still his response unsettled her. She said that she felt confused by his response, but I wonder if that confusion wasn't masking her own displeasure at her father's inability to properly protect her from her mother. She reported she did try to speak with him another time. His response then troubled her even more. He said nothing, simply frowned, raised an eyebrow, fell even more silent and withdrawn. It could very well be that his silence was a reflection of his own feelings of helplessness in regard to both the alcoholism of his wife and its effects on his daughter. The silence may have arisen from his not knowing what to say to Katie. His frown, his raised eyebrow may have been disapproval at his wife's behavior or at his own helplessness in the face of it. The reasons will never be known because he never talked about it. But Katie drew her own conclusions. His raised eyebrow, his frown and his withdrawal made her feel guilty of some terrible wrong that she did not understand. It seemed to have to do with looking to her father for protection or help in dealing with her mother. It seemed to have to do with attending to herself.

Focusing Off The Self

Bringing up the issue with her father and staying focused on herself and her needs, produced feelings of shame, disloyalty and guilt in Katie. She learned it was better not to focus on her own pain. She learned to endure the situations, having few alternatives. However, she could escape the *impact* of those situations and that is exactly what she did. She looked away from herself; she distanced herself from herself. She focused on situations, on others and on tasks. She avoided looking inward to what she thought, how she felt and what she saw. Life was measured by how others felt, what others thought and what others saw. The course of Katie's afternoon as a child depended not on what she did or how she felt when she arrived home from school each day but on how her mother felt. Having a snack depended not on Katie's hunger or desire for a snack but on the degree of intoxication of her mother. Getting a good night's sleep depended not on Katie's need for it but on how much her parents argued that night. Having a hot, nutritious dinner depended not on Katie's nutritional requisites but on whether her mother was sober enough to prepare it.

To look inward, to attend to what she needed and felt not only brought no satisfaction of her needs but also no outlet or relief for her feelings. Instead it brought with it additional feelings of shame, disloyalty and guilt, undefined but powerful messages about herself to herself. To survive meant to focus on others, to avoid feeling painful feelings; to avoid conflict because it never resolved adequately. To survive meant to look away, from feelings, from conflict and ultimately from the self.

A Compromised Strength

What are the results of this kind of inattention to the self, this denial of one's pain or feelings? When I met Katie she was twenty-four years old; she had long dark hair, pale white skin and large, pale blue eyes. She was also very thin and looked as delicate and fragile as an antique porcelain figurine. She had two young children, both under the age of three and a drug-addicted husband who made as many demands on her as her children. She did all the cleaning, cooking and child-rearing. He only worked sporadically so Katie also held down a part-time but very taxing job at a local mental health crisis center. In addition, she received no emotional support from her husband but rather had to endure his verbal abuse and total preoccupation with himself and his addiction. The delicacy of Katie's appearance was certainly no measure of her strength or ability to function. She performed admirably in multiple roles that many would have found impossible to maintain and she did so without a support system to sustain her.

Katie's "ability" to endure under such circumstances, to tolerate the intolerable, may be the ultimate result of her inattention to herself. What looks like a deeply-ingrained masochism may in fact be this almost total lack of attention to herself, her own needs and her own pain. Katie, when she describes her life, is aware of what she is doing but not emotionally connected to it. She blocks awareness of the impact of her impossible lifestyle on herself. It is not that she experiences gratification from the burdens she allows herself to endure, which would be masochistic, but rather that she does not allow herself to feel their weight. She does not see what her behavior does to her. She does not have a balanced appreciation of her limitations that allows her to say no to unreasonable demands on her. She does not anticipate the toll it will take when she agrees to take on one more task, one additional responsibility. The price Katie pays for surviving by looking away is dear. Significant and profound deficits in her capacity for self care result in a life of overwork with little reward, of service and sacrifice to others and an abnegation of her own healthy needs.

This is the life of a victim. Katie was in many ways a victim as a child. Her forever focusing outward perpetuates the position of victim in adulthood when it could be otherwise. Katie will never have a sound sense of herself as being in control of her life until she can focus on her power to affect her life rather than to just respond to what life has to bring her. Externalizing control while at the same time endlessly attempting to control the uncontrollable (that which comes from without, such as her husband's addiction) leaves her forever caught as the victim in a play she writes but does not realize she writes. If she could see her own authorship, she could then change the script to better suit what she wants and what she needs. She could see that she need no longer be a victim.

Lois was described earlier as the child who learned denial at her mother's knee, who learned not to look for the broken objects she heard crashing in the middle of the night when the next morning all signs of those sounds had been cleared away. She shows the same lack of attention to her own needs. When her addicted husband's behavior threatened to cause her pain, she became curiously incurious. When she made a series of sarcastic remarks about her husband, I asked her what she thought about her marriage. She replied, "On a scale of one to ten I'd give it a four." She was clearly indicating her displeasure but without being specific. In order to help her clarify what was displeasing her, I then asked what she would like from her husband. She looked at me blankly, clearly having no idea of what needs could be satisfied within the marriage. Attempts to help her identify what some of her needs might be and what her husband could do to meet them failed miserably. Lois manifested a vague but global dissatisfaction and no sense of how it could be better for her. She had no awareness of the satisfactions to be had or the needs not being fulfilled even though she clearly felt dissatisfied and unfulfilled.

Katie seems able to manage almost any hardship. But when it comes to looking inward, to experiencing emotional pain, to staying with interpersonal conflict, Katie crumbles. Even the gentlest of therapy sessions, if they entailed Katie looking at or talking about her feelings were almost intolerable for her. Tearfully she would attempt to end them precipitously by pleading, "I have to go home to my children. They need me." Clearly it was she who needed them, needed to focus on them and their needs so she would not have to face her own pain. She also endured her husband's drug addiction and all the discomfort it caused the family rather than confront him and run the risk of causing additional conflict in the relationship. She cannot see that avoiding the pain has prolonged it, even enlarged it because she does not use it to propel her to take appropriate measures to correct the situations causing her pain. Her very ability to endure compromises the quality of her life and prevents her from developing an inner strength that could ultimately help her to reduce duress.

Katie has admitted to an intense sensitivity to others. She acknowledged that she is usually far more aware of how her children or husband are feeling than how she is feeling. This attention to others makes one a good friend, spouse or therapist, but it has additional negative intrapsychic consequences. Katie has become so focused on others that she draws her entire valuation of herself from the way others think about her. She talked about how devastated she became when her husband criticized her. When I asked her why his criticism was so devastating she responded, "Because that's how I judge myself, by what he thinks of me. And by what other people think of me." She paused, searching my face intently, and then asked, "Isn't that what everybody does?" There was anxiety in her voice, as if my response would also somehow define her and pass judgment on her. This vision that never looks inward can therefore never reflect back to Katie the values and judgments that should have become internalized. Dependent on others to judge her and define her leaves Katie once again in the position of a victim whose well-being is dependent on the whims, the values and the prejudices of others.

The Inner Life

Once again I return to Mark and his dilemma. To have to choose between an oncoming train and an icy river to survive can be seen as metaphor for the impossible choices presented to children of alcoholism. These choices refer to both physical danger and psychological trauma. The metaphor also describes the quality of the parenting with which the child is forced to live. The oncoming train represents the overtly hostile and aggressive parent, in this case Mark's father. The icy river symbolizes the other parent's inability to properly nurture and provide safety for the child. In this case that is Mark's mother.

How is Mark to feel about his parents, about a father who is often physically or emotionally abusive and a mother who seems loving and concerned but who protected neither Mark nor herself from her husband's cruelty? Can Mark "choose" to feel his disappointment, his sadness, his rage at parents who were irresponsible and unresponsive to his needs? It was safer not to feel, to look away from the feelings and to ignore the inner life.

The configuration of abusive father and loving but unprotecting mother that Mark experienced is similar to Eli's parents. Eli's father was highly respected in the community but violently alcoholic in the home. As an adaptation to this, Eli also learned not to attend to his inner life. Eli used very few words to describe the childhood traumas he experienced and all those words were about others, not himself. He described how his father pushed his sister down a flight of stairs. He described how his father, mother and he all accompanied his sister to the emergency room of the local hospital. And how his father told the staff on admission that his daughter had fallen off a chair, and how his mother did not correct his father's story: "My mother was there, too. She didn't say a word! But she knew. And I knew, too." He did not describe the feelings one could be expected to feel in such a situation. Eli cannot describe those feelings because they are so unavailable to him. He focused not on himself at such a time but away from himself. The irony in his voice was reserved for judgment of his father and his mother and perhaps himself also, but judgment now, as an adult. It is a retrospective judgment which is not the same as the experiencing of feelings in the midst of such a situation.

But can Eli dare to feel or be aware of his feelings in such a situation? Eli is six years old and in an emergency room because his father has just pushed his sister down a flight of stairs. Eli has described his sister as the one who stood up to their father and who protected Eli from his father's wrath. As a result she sustained serious injuries. How can Eli stand up to his father? How can Eli express his feelings to his father? Tears, he has learned, only bring on more of his father's rage. And in instances like this, they do not elicit his mother's protectiveness. And so Eli describes the scene. And while, now in the safety of his adulthood, his voice expresses both the anger and the pain that one would expect such a memory to generate, when I ask him about feelings he had at the time he looks at me with puzzlement on his face, shakes his head and once again lapses into a deep silence.

Alicia is the young woman who bundled up her younger siblings and trotted miles through the snow to have Christmas with a friend when her parents did not come home from a night on the town on Christmas Eve. She is also the one who went to see the school principal for her brother and gave her sister a birthday party because her parents did not. She verbalizes the experience: "I never felt alone because I was taking care of my brother and sister. I never felt scared: I felt responsible." Alicia survived the disappointment of a cold and lonely Christmas by not feeling it, by not experiencing it, by looking to the needs of others and not to her own as the only way of getting through the terrible, unhappy times.

At the time and given the circumstances, it was probably the best thing to do, the most functional, the most self-preserving and the best way to take care of herself. Because it *is* a successful survival technique, it becomes deeply embedded within her character, unquestioned by her. Looking away never raises doubts or anxiety when she uses it as an adult in healthier situations where it may cause pain rather than relieve it. She admits that she is not good at getting her own needs met. But she cannot satisfy her own needs until she can look inward to see what those needs are. She also confesses that she allows herself to be used by others rather than say no to them because she feels saying no will produce conflict. Conflict is more intolerable for Alicia than living with her own needs unmet. Alicia, so capable of taking charge and taking control suddenly becomes the victim when taking charge or taking control is required to satisfy her own needs.

Emma who spoke of life-long suicidal urges, shows the same tendency to externalize and to distance herself from her inner life. While speaking of these impulses, she denies feeling sad or depressed and rejects empathic responses from me, perhaps because they will connect her with her feelings. When I mirror and name the feelings she is expressing, she rejects the mirroring. To deal with the suicidal urges, she works long hours and does rigorous physical exercise. She displaces her feelings onto her work or her body, never entertaining the thought that looking toward her feelings might help her to gain some control over them.

And finally, as I think of looking outward I think again of three-year-old Sally who looked so old and burdened as she told me that she could make her mother stop using drugs. I could not at the time understand why she looked so old. She was dressed like a normal three-year-old. She was not large for her age, quite the opposite. Her features were the features of a little girl. But something about her eyes and the expression on her face seemed so very old. Perhaps it had to do with how she focused her attention — so alert and so watchful of everything about her — looking for threat or danger and being on guard for it. She did not have the relaxed, dreamy, self-absorbed look of the young child. Nor did she show the naivete or wonder of the child free to explore her environment, with nothing more to hold her attention than the wonder of new things to see or new places to explore. Sally, as she quickly let me know, was ever watchful of her mother and for her mother, ever focused on her mother to protect her, take care of her. Perhaps it was that look that so changed Sally's face from that of fresh-looking, curious and innocent three-year-old to hyperalert, worried and vigilant old woman.

The
Adulthood

PART III

The Illusion:
Part II

Life in an alcoholic family is viewed through the distortions of denial, repression, minimization and avoidance. The alcoholic denies the alcoholism, minimizes the negative consequences of alcoholic drinking, represses feelings and thoughts about the unpleasant events surrounding the drinking and avoids, above all, confrontation or even definition of the problem. The sober parent often uses these same defenses in attempts to cope with the alcoholism. Both parents, unable to face the painful fact that their behavior is harmful to the children, deny not only the alcoholism, but also its effects on their children. This arises not from malevolence on the parents' part but from a false belief that if they do not talk about the addiction or acknowledge it, then their children will be spared its effects and the pain it causes.

The children are left with a series of conflicting messages, words from the parents that contradict what the children experience. They are told that Daddy is "just asleep" when he is in actuality passed out from drinking too much, or that Mommy is "not herself" when in fact she is drunk. The children's feelings about what they see and hear, are also impugned by the parents. "You shouldn't feel bad." "There's nothing to worry about." "It's not right to be angry." "Stop crying." These messages that adults recall from their childhood reflect the lack of validation from both parents. The parents' good intentions in minimizing the impact on the children also provide a double message. The children learn that deceit, which upsets and confuses them, is in certain instances well-intentioned by the parents.

Therefore, children of alcoholism live in a reality that, as defined by the parents, often contradicts what the children perceive. This contradiction leaves the children with significant conflicts vitiating their ability to accurately assess what they see and hear and think and feel. As adults, this may result in actual deficits in their ability to consistently assess reality accurately, particularly when their perceptions are challenged or are reminiscent of the old situations. Adults speak frequently about confusion whenever their perceptions are questioned or challenged. Confusion may be a misnomer because, when pressed, those same speakers often can acknowledge that they *did* know what they saw and heard, but that it *contradicted* what the parents told them. To affirm their perceptions would call into question either the validity of the parents' perceptions *or* the parents' honesty. There can be no "good" resolution of the dilemma thus posed to the children and confusion might be the safest of solutions.

The integrity of the children's perceived reality is further compromised by the inconsistency in parental behavior resulting from the alcoholism. Promises are sometimes broken and sometimes honored. Parents are sometimes honest and sometimes dishonest. Family life is sometimes peaceful and orderly and sometimes chaotic, violent and crisis-ridden. For the children the results are that life is not consistent, reliable or predictable.

Not only do the children live passively in an environment created and defined for them by the parents, they also take on some of the characteristics of their environment. If they learn that denial, minimization, repression and avoidance are ways to survive in a chaotic, frightening and unpredictable universe, then they, too will use such defenses to survive. Children begin to reflect their environment and their upbringing. They may begin to present themselves differently from how they really are.

This deceptiveness of appearances I call illusion because the image the child projects to the world may be false or misleading instead of an accurate representation of the person. Illusion is a presentation of the self to the world that deceives both the world and the self. This presentation is often one dimensional, not allowing for the paradox and complexity children grew up with but never learned to integrate. Illusion is usually based on the expectations of others rather than a reflection of the inner self. At times it is intentional, at other times unintentional, at times conscious and at other times unconscious. It develops as a means of survival and as a defense against the destruction of the self. Surviving in an alcoholic family often means that the children must practice major deceits: to say and do for the parents what they think the parents want them to say and do and to suppress their own needs and feelings in order to meet the needs of the parents. The children come to believe that they must ensure the parents' survival to ultimately ensure their own survival.

The illusion is not only a projection to the world, but to the self as well. It may be safer not to recognize one's own anger or sadness or fear if there is no safe environment in which to express such feelings. It may be safer not to recognize one's needs if they must be ignored in order to satisfy the parents' needs. It may feel safer to focus always on others more attentively than on the self. It may decrease inner conflict to neglect the self and be inattentive to the self so that one is not continuously faced with decisions as to whose needs should be met and whose neglected.

Although the illusion could be defined as the operation of various defense mechanisms or survival strategies, in actuality the phenomenon is more inclusive than any single description. To think of it in this comprehensive way can be more helpful to adult children of alcoholics, their significant others and their therapists. The illusion is a symbolic representation that points to a variety of experiences. Once one is alert to its presentation in a given area then it can be examined to determine what it specifically means in that situation.

Initially life supporting, the illusion eventually becomes destructive because it leads children to an increasing alienation from themselves. An inadequate awareness of their inner lives inevitably leaves them feeling phony or unauthentic and thus undeserving of hard-earned praise or rewards for accomplishments. Focusing only on doing or saying what will please or satisfy others, leaves them with a sense of inadvertently putting something over on others and of never being satisfied or understood by others. It leaves them doubting what their true feelings are. Finally, it leaves them questioning their own identities and never really being sure of who they are.

My clinical observations indicate that it is misleading to think about children of alcoholism without accounting for the illusion. This illusion, this response to an inexplicable, irrational and unpredictable reality, surrounds both the external and the internal presentation of the child. Externally, such children and later such adults, look either better or worse to others than they really are. They look more in control than they may feel or more out of control than they actually are; more organized, efficient and capable or more scattered, chaotic and disorganized than is in fact the reality. To the world they may appear more successful or more maladjusted than actually is the case. To the therapist, they may seem to have more or less ego strength, a more or less severe diagnosis and to have made better or worse adaptations than may be true.

In my experience this illusion, whether it be masking inner or outer phenomena, always seems to be present, seems often to deceive, and as such affects not only children of alcoholism but also those with whom they interact. Whether it be loved ones, friends, employers, employees or co-workers, when the illusion is operating expectations are unrealistic because they are based on the illusion. Therefore, people will be disappointed or confused because children of alcoholism perform either above or below their apparent capabilities, or in contrast to their stated intentions.

Employers might expect, for example, that they be more or less responsible than they present themselves at work; spouses or friends might expect them to be more or less open and honest than they present themselves in a relationship. They may be more or less committed to work, to a friendship or to therapy than they appear to be. The illusion often leaves spouses or lovers and children confused as to the mixed messages they receive, particularly around communication, the desire for intimacy and conflict resolution. The illusion often leaves therapists puzzled as to why certain highly motivated, seemingly hard-working and insightful people precipitously leave treatment. It also may leave therapists perplexed when they see people who have had seemingly good previous treatment over long periods of time remain with certain key issues, very problematic issues, apparently untouched. The illusion also leaves adult children of alcoholics perplexed as to why they do not feel better or function better, or why they continue to repeat old patterns after extensive therapy. In addition, adult children of alcoholics may assign to their therapists an omniscience they do not possess, expecting them to see beneath the illusion when this is not always possible.

Where this illusion begins and how early it begins is probably situational, dependent on the internal and external circumstances of the family's life during the various phases of the child's development. However it seems clear that the illusion is a response to these circumstances. That the creation and maintenance of an illusion is both response and adaptation to living in a home with an active addiction also seems clear. The extent of the illusion as well as its depth and its permeation of the child's character may be determined by how early the need for it arose in the child's life and by the severity of the situation that maintained it. But my clinical experience indicates that the illusion exists, in one form or another, if one grew up in a home with an actively alcoholic parent.

The illusion manifests itself in many ways. It is a reflection and perpetuation of the early life. It also is reflected in the way people appear, the way they structure family life and communicate with each other and the way they structure their relationships as caretakers. The illusion is so pervasive that it has a major influence on how people organize the inner sense of the self and their identity.

Appearances

Sean's Story

Sean typifies this misleading presentation of the self. Sean both *is* and is *never* as he appears to be. Handsome, articulate and personable he appears the perfect image of a successful professional and a devoted family man. Now a grandfather in his late fifties, he looks in fine health, without a care in the world. It is not readily apparent that his health has been seriously compromised by years of alcoholic drinking and that the charming, self-assured smile masks ongoing fears, anger and near-paralyzing insecurity.

On first impression, he appears to be the modern Renaissance man: first a successful journalist and then a politician and entrepreneur. Hidden are the reasons for the various and varied careers that indicate he might not be as versatile as he seems. Also hidden is the fact that the apparent successes are compromised by such financial and personal mismanagement that he is on the verge of financial ruin.

Clearly a devoted family man, he speaks with sensitivity about his four grown children and his wife of 30 years. When one hears him speak with such love of his family, it is not apparent how devastating his alcoholism has been to each one of them and how they too have now developed serious symptoms as a result. One son is socially withdrawn, with severe allergies and frequent psychosomatic illnesses; a daughter is married to an alcoholic; and his wife is struggling with her own addiction to tranquilizers and sleeping pills.

Sean's memories of his childhood are filled with the same contradictory images he projects. He speaks of his father with a mixture of pride and disgust. His father was alcoholic as far back as Sean can remember. When drinking his father would often fly into rages, throw things, break things and hurl vicious verbal disparagements at his wife and children. He would berate his family as no good, curse at them, devalue them and claim he drank because of them. The relationship was not all anger and disparagement, however. Love and pride were there also. But Sean remembers the love and pride always being intertwined so that one must question how conditional that love may have felt to Sean. Did his father only love him when Sean made him proud? Sean had only one memory he was able to share as example of his father's love. His father took Sean to his favorite bar with him to show him off to his drinking buddies; he glowed with pride as he said, "My son will become a U.S. senator or maybe even president some day." Although Sean shook his head in disapproval as he recalled his father's bragging, there was a sense of yearning commingled with the disapproval, as if Sean wished he could satisfy his father, live up to his father's unrealistic expectations of him and also perhaps cure his father of his alcoholism.

Contradictory emotions seem always to be a part of Sean's memories. When Sean describes his past his face twists in disgust as he remembers his father's physical and verbal violence and his repeated failures as a breadwinner. At other times pride replaces repugnance as he describes his father as a blue-collar worker and an immigrant with no formal education who taught himself to read and write, devouring the classics and reading books on philosophy the way his neighbors read comic books. While drinking partners at his local tavern read the daily tabloid, Sean's father read the daily *New York Times*. Sean clearly admired his father's ability and drive to rise above his untutored origins and to pursue his love of knowledge in spite of his environment. But when this is mentioned, the admiration on his face quickly disappears and he denies any such feelings about his father. Is this part of Sean's illusion about himself, that he only hates his father? Does the denial of the admiration and need to please his father allow him to unconsciously attempt to satisfy his father's needs at the expense of his own needs?

Sean went away to college, happy to be away from home at last. Like his father he loved literature and writing and eventually became a journalist despite his father's desire for a famous politician. He loved his work and was good at it, gradually working his way toward better and better positions. But Sean did not feel that these successes satisfied his father. Pressured by his father, he went into local politics. This meant he had to give up his writing. To support himself and his family, and as a result of his political connections, he gradually got into various business ventures that finally took up most of his time. He never liked business or politics and felt he was not good at them. Although adamant about his dislike of his current activities and his lack of talent there, he is vague about why he gave up his writing.

And so Sean, denying any desire or need to fulfill his .father's fantasies or to win approval from his father, attempted to nonetheless. He abandoned a career that was satisfying for one in which he felt neither competent nor satisfied. And he is not clear, to others or to himself, why he did it.

The illusion is further enacted in the contrasts between his work performance and his personal life. As a result of the work he did in his political ward, he eventually became a local entrepreneur, bringing together the various participants in business ventures. He became a negotiator for clients having problems with their mortgages and the mortgagor. But, he let his own mortgage come close to foreclosure as he not only let himself fall six months behind in his payments but then took no steps to protect himself or negotiate with the bank. The skills he could use for his clients suddenly disappeared when he needed them for himself. Although this phenomenon is certainly not unique to children of alcoholism, the illusion surrounding the phenomenon is often associated with the consequences of growing up in an alcoholic household. It is also the illusion surrounding his abilities that confuses and angers his family as they experience the anxiety of imminent foreclosure. It is the illusion to himself that prevents him from coming to grips with a problem that he consciously disowns but unconsciously perpetuates. He allows the illusion of his own competence to betray him, to give him a false sense of security. His skill as a negotiator, and his ability to rescue clients from the brink of foreclosure become illusory when applied to himself and his own home because he does not face his inability to be self-protective and to follow through by negotiating and advocating for himself.

When Sean's son was a senior in high school, he expressed a desire to go to an out-of-town college. Sean was determined that his son feel free to make his own choice around all aspects of his college life, particularly because Sean had felt so manipulated by his own father. Yet Sean recalls that his son was almost refused admittance because Sean kept putting off sending in the tuition and dormitory deposit. Again, Sean could not muster his own resources to accomplish what in other circumstances would be a simple task. Because he was unaware of his own ambivalence, he could not struggle with it, account for it or work through it; instead he played it out.

Ostensibly, Sean's professional performance was outstanding. But again, behind closed doors, the picture was very different. Although he helped clients organize and manage their affairs, his own office was in shambles; important documents were strewn about, unfiled and with records poorly and erratically kept. His office can be seen as a reflection of his inner life — disorganized, chaotic and near collapse. In contrast, his appearance, the image he presents to the world is always meticulous.

In describing his dilemma Sean said, "The things you do on the outside, like reading the *New York Times* and being a respectable business man and politician, are different from what you are on the inside." He allows us to see behind the facade as if to make the point. Dressed in a professional looking navy pin-striped three-piece suit and carrying an elegant attache case, he opened the case (which was supposed to be carrying important papers) to reveal only a newspaper and a book of word games.

Family Life

The same contradictions apply in Sean's family life. Grimly determined not to become like his father, he does anyway. Speaking with a passion of the havoc his father's alcoholism wreaked on the entire family and speaking tenderly about his deep love for his family, he became alcoholic and wreaked the same havoc on his own family. His wife also had an alcoholic parent. Conflicts around caretaking were often unresolvable because they both struggled consciously to be independent of each other and unconsciously to be taken care of by the other. Thus, dependency becomes another arena in which the illusion presents itself.

The role of caretaker is key for most children of alcoholism. Being a caretaker to others assumes a certain ability to act autonomously and independently and to take charge and take control. Caretaking may also frequently represent an avoidance of feelings of being dependent, vulnerable and out-of-control. And yet often, buried deep within the caretaker, is the profound desire to be cared for, to be dependent and passive with an all-nurturing other who will care for the caretaker, totally and unconditionally. Self-sufficiency and independence become part of the illusion when they are used to mask these powerful tendencies toward passivity and dependency. Although it is not uncommon for people to have conflicting feelings around being cared for and taking care of, it is again the illusion, the need to keep these conflicts hidden from others and from the self, that makes them particularly untouchable. Sean and his wife endlessly played out their conflicts around dependence and caretaking. Their lack of awareness of the deeper issues prevented them from ever resolving these conflicts. This led them to continuously precipitate household crises as each waited for the other to take care of paying the bills, making necessary household repairs and balancing the checkbook.

Speaking with disdain of the verbal abuse he and his mother endured when his father drank, Sean, too, became verbally abusive when he drank. He showered his wife and children with the same verbal attacks he experienced from his father. The incident with his oldest son's college tuition was typical of the kinds of interaction Sean described with his family. He knew he had to send in the tuition money and dormitory deposit by a certain date to insure his son's place and he knew what the deadline was. He also spoke with tenderness and absolute sincerity about his determination that his son have the kind of education he wanted without being subject to the manipulations he experienced from his father.

Nevertheless, Sean procrastinated about sending in the tuition money and dormitory room deposit just as he procrastinated about other important financial matters regarding the family. "It wasn't that I didn't want to. It wasn't that I couldn't afford to," he said, regarding the money, "I kept promising him that I would. And I never did." The apparent desire for his son to have the education he wanted was belied by his procrastination. His promises seem sincere but were in reality shallow and empty. He repeated his father's pattern despite his sincere determination not to. He no more acted in the best interests of his son than did his father. While again, this kind of behavior is not limited to children of alcoholism, Sean's blindness to the hidden motives that drive him keep him from changing behavior that is contrary to what he consciously desires for his son. His behavior also is contrary to his wish to be the generous and supportive father that his father was not. Sean's inability to change his behavior put his son in a position that was reminiscent of the earlier generation — enraged at his father for sabotaging his entrance into college but with no way to express that rage because of Sean's denial of his hostile behavior. For no matter what his conscious experience or intention, Sean's behavior is sadistic. Sean cannot acknowledge his sadism and his ambivalence toward his son. This nonverbal, disavowed behavior has more devastating effects on his son than overt, verbal attacks because double messages, nonverbal behavior that contradicts the verbal, cannot be confronted or resolved.

Communication

This incident also illustrates the extent to which communication becomes compromised with Sean. Sean's father told him that he loved him, had high expectations of him then cursed him, cruelly criticized him, used Sean's career to bolster his own shattered self-esteem in the face of his business failures. Sean received conflicting messages from his father.

Sean in turn gives conflicting messages to his son. He told his son, *and meant it* at the time, that he wanted him to go to college. Then Sean did not send out the tuition in time. He repeatedly promised that he would and then did not. The messages were conflicting. Sean berates his father for never talking to him and proudly insists that he and his children do talk. But to what avail if speech has no integrity and if it belies the behavior? Speech then for Sean's son is deceitful, not to be trusted, in fact to be guarded against. It is not just Sean's words, but the sincerity behind them that creates the illusion.

There is another form of illusion that involves Sean's speech. Sean uses words to hide rather than reveal himself, to escape rather than face his circumstances, to avoid rather than experience and work through his pain. He talks instead of acting and the talk becomes a way to act out unacknowledged feelings. Stories entertain and distract the listener but they also enable Sean to keep his distance, to avoid closeness or significant self-revelation to another human being. Although this feels like protection against an intimacy he fears, it isolates Sean, keeps him alone with his words and his stories. His eloquence too is illusion.

The Inner Life

The illusion in this case is not only an interactional phenomenon with Sean's son but an internal event as well. Sean appears impassive as he describes the tuition incident. He seems unaware of his own ambivalence regarding his son's college attendance.

This lack of awareness keeps him as confused by his behavior as it must keep his son.

This lack of ability for introspection is not readily apparent. Fluent, articulate, even passionate in his presentation, Sean could be spellbinding with his stories. In therapy, he could mesmerize the members of the therapy group with his apparent ability to describe himself and his history and to relate it to some of the personality characteristics of adult children of alcoholics that he had been reading about. As his stories went on week after week with only the content changing, it became evident that he was using his fine ability to articulate as defense; his words kept him from his feelings; his dramatic presentation kept him from doing more than merely describing his memories.

The apparent insight is illusory, masking great gaps in his ability to self-observe. When he is able to acknowledge certain characteristics as applying to himself, he could not then go beyond superficial identification or intellectualization. After a time he began to recognize at least some aspect of this. "You know," he said with a sad expression on his face, "I had hoped I'd be able to cry about this. But I haven't." Sean's inability to experience his feelings leads to another facet of the illusion.

The Ultimate Caretaker

Sean went into politics not because he wanted to but because he thought it was what his father wanted. This is reminiscent of the children in Chapter 4, "The Caretaker: Part I." Those children saw themselves, one from as early as age three, as caretakers of their parents, not only responsible for the performance of tasks around the house and control of the parental alcoholism but also for the very well-being of the parent. In such instances they believe they have to suppress all but their most basic needs to satisfy the needs of their vulnerable parents. Their own feelings also have to be repressed in order to care for the needy parents.

Lives in those homes are not organized around the children's needs but around the consequences of the alcoholic drinking. These consequences are so compelling that the children do not get the kind of attention they need from their parents. They do not get the age-appropriate nurturing that they need to develop a secure and positive sense of themselves. In addition, they may become so aware of the (apparent) fragility of the parents (the sober one as well as the alcoholic) that emotionally they reverse roles and see themselves as responsible for the parents' well-being. Sean provides an example of this use of the self to care for the parents. Before looking further at Sean it may be helpful to look more specifically at how caretaking feeds the illusion.

A drunken father cannot take his son to a Little League game, even though he had sincerely promised and intended to when he was sober. The son, seeing his father hung over Saturday morning might tell his father that the game has been cancelled or slip out of the house early, before his father has begun to "treat" the hangover with more alcohol. He thus spares himself and his father the embarrassment of his father's appearing with him at the game either drunk or irritable from the hangover. A mother who sneaks a drink every time there is stress in the home cannot be an empathic support for her daughter who has just flunked a history test. In fact, the daughter might try to hide her grade just so as not to upset her mother and cause her to drink even more.

This is the raw material that illusions are made of. The little boy hides his disappointment from the other team members by bravado or silence. This is the external expression of the illusion. If such incidents happen often enough and he has no outlet for the disappointment he might begin to hide the disappointment from himself as a way to cope with it. This is the internal manifestation of the illusion, the alienation from his own inner life.

The little boy may also interpret his father's overinvolvement with the alcohol and underinvolvement with him as a reflection of the son's assumed unworthiness. His self-esteem, already low from lack of attention and interest by the parents, will be lowered even further by his feelings of being unloved and unlovable. All the more reason, then, to try to look good and to prove to the world, but especially to his father, just how talented he is. And maybe, if he's really good, he reasons, if he can come home and tell his dad that he hit the winning home run, maybe then his dad will be so proud he'll stop drinking. And maybe then, he hopes, he will feel better about himself. All the more reason, then, to tighten the illusion around him, to look better, to do better as his father continues to drink and he continues to experience the father's drinking as his own failure, as a reflection of his own inadequacy. The son is centered not on himself but on his father; his successes are for his father; his self-worth is determined by whether or not his father stops drinking. The boy sees not *his* moods but his father's, not *his* dreams but his father's. This focus on the father, this centering outside the self also helps to maintain the illusion because it enables the boy not to look at himself.

And the little girl who has just flunked a test and feels terrible about it — where can she go with those feelings? When her mom is "normal" (not drinking), she smiles at the little girl, at her prettiness, her sweetness; she enjoys dressing her in beautiful clothes and brushing her long, silky hair. But when the little girl scrapes her knee and it bleeds and she cries, the mother tenses, withdraws, becomes clumsy and abrupt in her attempts to tend the injury. Her self-esteem and belief in her competence to be an adequate mother are already very low. Her attention is more often on the bottle than on her daughter. Her parenting is more often dictated by her own needs than providing for her daughter. Whether this is the cause or effect of the alcoholism, for her daughter the effects are the same, a mother who is not consistently there for her daughter. The little girl can never be sure whether her tears cause her mother to tense and then to reach for the bottle. But when her mother drinks she withdraws from the child and becomes inaccessible to her. It becomes safer to hide the tears, to remain only pretty and sweet as much as possible. It becomes safer to hide the flunked test and the feelings that go with it, not only from her mother, but eventually from herself. Looking the way her mother wants her to look, and for the boy behaving the way his father wants him to behave, may eventually be perceived as the only way to be cared for or attended to. These behaviors become deeply connected with survival. Thus, surviving becomes hiding one's true self; surviving becomes serving others to the abnegation of the self.

This may be the phenomenon that Sean reflected as he went into politics. It would appear, from the way Sean tells this story, that he experienced his father's love as conditional and that those conditions had to do with what his father *wanted* rather than what Sean *was.* To get his father's approval, then, Sean will be forced into a compliance with his father's wishes. He will have to sacrifice his own needs (as he did by abandoning his career as a journalist) to satisfy his needy father.

Sean views his mother as far more benign and nurturing. But her behavior also reinforces the notion that Sean is there to meet his parents' needs before his own. Sean's mother, who hated bars, also sent Sean to them to fetch his father when he stayed too long. At those times Sean was not the recipient of his father's pride but rather of his belligerence as roles reversed and son had to bring father safely home. Sean's mother was sending Sean into both the hated environment of the bar, sacrificing his safety to ensure the safety of her husband and also sacrificing Sean's well-being as she placed him in the position of being the recipient of his father's belligerence. Sean was not consciously aware of the message of his mother, which *appeared* benign to Sean, but unfortunately it was the same message he had received from his father: The needs of others come before one's own. No wonder Sean gave up his beloved journalism career so easily in the face of his father's displeasure with it!

Alienation From The Self

Becky as an adult demonstrates the results of years of not experiencing feelings. She insists that it wasn't so bad growing up with her alcoholic mother. It slips out that holiday meals were usually anywhere from one to four hours late. She knew those were not the only late meals, but those were the ones that made her choke back the tears as she remembered them. Again she repeats, "It wasn't that bad," and this proclamation seems to help her regain her composure. She proceeds in a somewhat controlled but predominantly matter-of-fact voice to describe her first date in early adolescence. When I ask Becky what that was like, she sucks in her breath and answers softly, "Oh, I don't know. I guess I was a little embarrassed. I don't really remember." She then quickly changes the subject. Perhaps this was to spare herself the pain of such a memory or possibly it was to avoid acknowledging that she really had no idea of how she felt or that she had no memory of having any feelings at the time. Vagueness seems to shroud her memory of the incident. It is unclear whether this vagueness protects her from her emotion or hides the lack of it from herself.

Becky is a talented novelist, a writer of psychological fiction who deals in the language of feelings, who makes her living from it. She is articulate and apparently insightful as she turns her talent also on herself and her behavior. She struggles endlessly with words and with current theories in popular psychology to explain to herself her actions, her reactions and her interactions with the important people in her life. Her words indicate a mastery that her tone of voice and the look in her eyes belies. As she brushes against the old memories a flicker of pain crosses her face and she, who usually carefully explores her every thought and feeling, quickly pulls back.

Is this a reflection of Becky's alienation from her self? Does the studied, endless self-examination point to a search that Becky does not admit to, a search for something hidden beneath the carefully selected words and theories that she so painstakingly puts together?

At times Becky demonstrates a rage when she talks about her ex-husband that she never shows when she speaks about her mother. And yet, her mother's behavior was far more abusive to Becky than her husband's. When she speaks of her mother, it is usually to describe her as being extremely fragile. In describing her mother's outrageous behavior, Becky shows her frustration, but also a helplessness and protectiveness in the face of her mother's vulnerability. Given her belief in her mother's fragility, were Becky as a child, to have felt rage at her inattentive mother, such feelings might easily have overwhelmed her. Because Becky had nowhere to express her rage, to turn for comfort or to feel secure she ignored her own needs. Better to ignore such feelings, to deny them, safer not to recognize the existence of such feelings. The danger comes from within as well as without. The feelings of rage are as much a threat to her survival as the lack of adequate mothering. This survives into adulthood. Becky is no longer dependent on her mother but treats her as the same disappointing, demanding woman who evokes a rage she dare not express and who still evokes that insatiable longing to be cared for and nurtured. Still unaware of the power and complexity of her feelings, Becky continues to pose as the dutiful but distressed and oppressed daughter, torn by feelings she cannot acknowledge or relinquish.

This may be the dearest price that Becky and Sean pay for their survival: the loss of the awareness of their inner lives and the loss of the ability to perceive themselves clearly. Both their inner and outer realities become threats that they must defend against rather than riches to be sought after and enjoyed.

Sean, unaware of his past and present conflicting feelings about his family, plays out those feelings over and over again. Determined *not* to become alcoholic like his father, he becomes alcoholic. Determined *not* to try to please his father, he gives up a fulfilling career *for* his father. Determined to be a loving husband and parent, he abuses his wife and children. Unhappy with his life and wanting to change, instead he repeats. Intellectually acknowledging his own destructive and self-destructive behavior, emotionally he blames circumstance and others for what he does. While verbally taking responsibility for his actions, emotionally and behaviorally he remains a victim, trapped in the psyche of a helpless little boy.

Trapped By The Illusion

Theresa's Story

I end this chapter with Theresa for she illustrates how successful the illusion can be.

I met Theresa when her teenage son Tony became an inpatient as a result of his drug abuse. In my first interview with Theresa and her husband John I learned that Theresa's father had been an alcoholic. Theresa mentioned this matter-of-factly and firmly denied it had impacted on her except to give her added strength of character. By the way she sat and her tone of voice she made it very clear to me no more questions were to be asked about her history. It also came out that John's father was alcoholic. John presented himself as charming, low-keyed and seemingly more available than his wife. But John's availability also was illusory for he offered no more information than did Theresa about himself and never reappeared for further interviews or participation in the family program despite his promises to do so.

Theresa, a learning disabilities specialist, is in her late thirties. She exudes an air of complacency, even smugness. Social amenities fade into a brisk manner which soon shifts, as we discuss her son and his problem, to reveal someone who is quite rigid in her problem-solving abilities. Although she would be the first to deny it, the more she discusses the dilemmas she faces, the more she appears to be angry and controlling. She speaks in a slow, clipped manner, as if to a troublesome, tiresome young child.

John let Theresa do most of the talking in that first interview. The more relaxed and cooperative John appeared, the more intense and resistant Theresa became. He said enough about himself to reveal that he was bringing in a six-figure income while constantly on the brink of financial disaster because of his increasing tendency to make high-risk real estate investments. His cavalier attitude seemed to minimize the seriousness of his risk taking as he made it clear that he had lost hundreds of thousands of dollars. However, it was Theresa who carried all the anxiety for his behavior. She described John as a compulsive gambler. He half-admitted, half-denied this, but with such charm and low-key style that it was Theresa who "looked bad" — confronting, exaggerating and hostile. It was easy to overlook the fact that it was his behavior and not Theresa's that was threatening the family's financial security.

As they described their relationship it unfolded that Theresa attempted to control her husband's spending in much the same way her mother had attempted to control her father's drinking. But Theresa denied any similarities between her mother's behavior and her own. Citing her mother's utter failure to control her father's drinking, Theresa adamantly insisted that it was only because of her unceasing attempts to control John's investments that the family was not already financially ruined. John, a sheepish smile adding to his charm, half-heartedly concurred.

Theresa here compulsively plays back again and again her childhood and the denial that enables her to continue to act without having to acknowledge the repetitiveness of her behavior. As an adult she always remains on the brink, recreating the chaos and crises of her childhood while at the same time she denies it. Her assertion that she is saving the family from financial ruin indicates some very faulty reasoning that may keep her locked into repetitive self-destructive behavior. She implies that by avoiding financial ruin she is controlling her husband's gambling, that she has it in her power to control her husband's behavior, when in fact she does not. She keeps one step ahead of his spending, but she does not control the spending which is addictive and out-of-control. However, she does not allow herself to see this. What other motivations might she fail to see? Is she unconsciously trying to outdo her mother? Is she trying to master old failures — such as not curing her father — by the unending attempt to cure her husband? Is she comforting herself with the familiar, recreating the old family scene that is comfortable simply because it is familiar? It is not possible to answer with any certainty whether one or all of these possibilities apply. Only Theresa can explore the meanings of her behavior and her motivations. Unfortunately, Theresa is caught in the illusion here, much of it denial in this instance, of a life that is different from her childhood when in actuality it is not. The illusion traps her and leads her to endlessly repeat the old patterns.

John, too, perpetuates the illusion while at the same time becoming victim of it. They both allow him to play the good guy; both smile indulgently at his gambling. This allows him never to take seriously the gravity of his behavior nor to take responsibility for it. Was this how John's father was treated in his family and is John, too, unconsciously playing out old scenes with no under-standing or control over his actions?

Theresa had also tried to control her son Tony's addiction, with even less success. She had attended Al-Anon, the self-help group for families of alcoholics; she learned from them, at least superficially, that his addiction was his responsibility and that she could neither cure it nor control it. Although she gave lip service to those ideas she continued to attempt to exercise such control. Rejecting my attempts to join with her, to help her connect with her own sense of helplessness in the face of Tony's addiction, instead she took an aggressive, defensive position when her tendencies to take charge were pointed out to her. She took the same stance regarding recommendations for her son's posthospital care when they did not conform with what she had decided was right for Tony and her family. Because of Tony's already long history of drug abuse reaching back to the beginnings of his adolescence and because of his inability to set any limits on his own behavior or to abide by the limits his parents had attempted to set for him, it was recommended that Tony enter a long-term residential treatment program for teenage substance abusers. Predictably, Tony did not want this. Theresa joined Tony and vigorously fought our recommendations. As angry and disgusted as she claimed to be over Tony's inability to manage his life and as furious as she was at his refusal to let *her* manage his life, she suddenly gave in to his resistance to the plan, a plan that offered genuine hope for his recovery.

She joined Tony in his resistance. Rather than see myself and other staff as allies, she instead regarded us as the enemy. She rejected all attempts to engage her in a therapeutic alliance and accused us of not listening to her when we did not agree with her or do as she demanded. As time for Tony's discharge neared and staff members did not alter their recommendations to conform to what Theresa wanted, her posture became even more rigid, angry and condescending. She seemed to dismiss us as incompetent and uncaring.

During Tony's hospitalization she had been regularly attending a therapy group for the families of the patients. In the group the illusion had taken another form. Here she presented herself consistently as in compliance with our philosophy, knowledgeable of the principles of Al-Anon and applying them appropriately to her situation. She acted like a third therapist in the group and other members began to turn to her as an expert. Although she sounded compliant and agreeable, she kept it well hidden that she was bitterly opposing our recommendations for her son and acting as if we were nothing more than insensitive and incompetent meddlers. Attempts consistently failed to help her use the group in a more useful way to problem-solve some of the dilemmas she faced. She repeatedly gave advice, lectured and seemed smug and self-satisfied instead of identifying with other members' fear, insecurity and uncertainty.

This is a fairly typical use of the illusion for children of alcoholism, who frequently feel inadequate and are ashamed of themselves and their feelings. The more helpless and out-of-control they feel, the more they will project the image of being in control, composed and ready to meet any emergency. Whether this facet of the illusion is conscious or unconscious with a particular person or at a particular moment can only be determined by careful examination with that person. Theresa would not let us close enough to discover the nature of her illusion. My awareness that this posture served as defense against her own fear and insecurity, and that she was not ready to give up such defenses, led me to try to help her to use the group in another way that might be more productive for her. I encouraged her to share her dissatisfaction and anger at the staff (as other group members do at times), to get some help and input from the group. She would not do this and she did not seem to be making good use of the group. She seemed unable to avail herself of the support that the group is so good at providing, because she could not let them see her vulnerability and her suffering.

I wondered why she continued to come. On the one hand it seemed as if she only came to the group to prove what a good mother she was. On the other hand, even though it was not apparent, there seemed to be something more bringing her back regularly despite her displeasure with us. I wondered if she needed to prove to herself what a good mother she was, or if perhaps there was still something else . . .

At the time there were two other members of the group who had alcoholic parents. Although each had mentioned this, neither had elaborated on the parental alcoholism. Theresa had not referred to her father at all, but she always sat next to one of these two women and seemed to listen with particular attentiveness when either of them spoke. Because Theresa lived at a great distance from the hospital, she was not expected to take advantage of the four postdischarge sessions offered to members of the group. Surprisingly, she appeared the week after Tony was discharged. Again she rather self-righteously let the group know how well things were going and again presented herself as self-contained, inapproachable and in control.

The following week Theresa returned again. On this particular week, as is often the case, there was a radical change in group membership. A chronically alcoholic woman in her late fifties had just been admitted to the rehabilitation program. Her five young adult children came pouring into the group. Normally reticent, if not totally silent about their mother's drinking, their tongues became loosened by the pressures of the current crisis that brought their mother (now near death) into treatment. They spoke of their unsuccessful attempts over the years to get treatment for their mother.

Moved by the intensity of their suffering, other members of the group began to talk about long-standing feelings of helplessness, anger, guilt and inadequacy as they unceasingly and unsuccess-fully struggled to get their loved ones to stop drinking. One woman described her father's drinking and then with great poignancy admitted that she always thought it was because of her that he drank. She had never admitted this to anyone before. Another woman, with tears in her eyes, admitted to the group for the first time that her father had been an alcoholic. This might not seem like a particularly deep or meaningful revelation, but it was for her and those with whom she shared it. The disclosure increased the sense of closeness and trust in one another and encouraged more openness. One after another, members poured out to each other the old fears, the current anxieties and the endless unsuccessful struggles with their alcoholic parents. The room was charged with feeling as well as with a penetrating stillness that was punctuated only by the soft, almost breathless speech of one person after another.

Suddenly we heard a childlike cry. It was Theresa. Silent up to that point she now, through her tears, began to talk of how devastating her father's alcoholism had been for her. Sobbing, she described how inadequate, guilt-ridden and out-of-control she had felt as a child. Gone was the smugness, the rigidity, even the anger. She could barely speak through her tears. For the first time she seemed able to take comfort and support from others. They paralleled her stories with similar ones of their own and in that way they took her in, cut through her isolation and self-containment. Her defenses lowered enough for her to momentarily drop the facade she used to protect herself from her terrible self-image and overwhelming emotions. She allowed herself to face how utterly ashamed and inadequate she had felt during most of her life.

Theresa could not give up the illusion easily or quickly. It took weeks of experiencing the group as safe, nonconfronting and noncritical. Even then she could not reveal herself until after she heard other people describing experiences of their own that she thought were unique to her. Those experiences had so ravaged her self-image that she had buried them, hidden them even from herself beneath a facade of anger, smugness and self-righteousness. In individual sessions my attempts to join her, to empathize with her and to get her to recall some of her past had only intensified the defenses. However, hearing others who came out of a similar experience voice the same feelings released the previously repressed memories. In that short space of time Theresa was able to touch her own vulnerability without it seeming destructive or life-threatening.

What Theresa might choose to do with that experience is up to her. She might find relief from expressing old pains that continue to plague her even though they are out of her awareness most of the time. She might find comfort from the empathic response she received from others in the group. If she continued to be open and honest, she might get feedback from the group that would help her to understand herself better and possibly lead to the kinds of behavior changes that would improve the quality of her experiences with her husband and son.

However, Theresa has wrapped herself in the protective cloak of illusion for all of her adulthood and much of her childhood. She will not necessarily give it up because she has one or two good experiences with self-revelation. She may try to convince herself that those brief experiences are enough to bring about significant change, to increase her self-esteem and to decrease the overuse of the illusion as defense. But this is more illusion. Theresa returned to the group one more time. While the smugness and hostility seemed to be gone, this time she was very quiet. She said little about herself and what she said was relatively superficial. Whether she needed that last group to consolidate the work she had done the week before and to prepare for embarking on further work in her hometown or whether she was rebuilding her defenses around herself, I had no way of knowing.

CHAPTER 9

The Caretaker
Part II

"I felt older as a kid than I do now."
"I had so little control over so much."
"I never felt alone because I was taking care of my brother and sister.
I never felt scared. I felt responsible."

These are the words of thirty-six-year-old Alicia as she thinks about her childhood. Alicia described how she cared for her siblings when her parents were so preoccupied with their drinking that they had no time to make a birthday party for Alicia's sister, or go to school for her brother when he got into trouble or to be home Christmas morning when the children awoke.

Alicia took care of her sister's birthday party, she went to see the school principal for her brother and she made sure they all celebrated Christmas by getting herself and her brother and sister, on foot and in the snow, to a friend's house three miles away.

Alicia is an example of a child thrust into the role of caretaker at an early age. She demonstrates how that role, combined with the tendency to look always outward, toward others and the environment rather than inward and towards herself, results in the use of certain defenses and interactional patterns in adulthood. Her story is strikingly similar to others we've heard.

Her father was alcoholic, verbally and physically abusive to her mother. When asked if he was violent with the children she said, "No, unless we tried to break up their fights." This double message reflected her own confused perceptions of her father. He was violent to the children if they tried to interfere with his conflicts with their mother. This means he was violent. In connecting the violence with the children's behavior, she relieved him of the responsibility for his own violence and placed it instead on the children. This is a misperception, the kind of distorted thinking that leads not only to assuming responsibility for another's behavior but also to attempts to control that behavior.

Alicia describes her father as "always angry" except when not drinking and then "he didn't exist; he showed no feelings." Not existing is Alicia's way of describing his unavailability to her. No feelings means he showed no love, or interest in her. She also adds, "the only praise I ever received from him was when he was drinking." This sets her up to feel ambivalent about her father's drinking. As many terrible consequences as the drinking had for her and her family, it also had a very significant benefit; it enabled him to praise her. A parent's pride is as sustaining and important to a child as food and water. If the only way Alicia is to receive a sign of her father's pride is through his drinking, then as much as she hates his drinking, she also desires it. She might not be consciously aware of her ambivalence, but this does not mean it does not have significant influence on her.

She is not sure whether or not her mother is alcoholic, but thinks she only drank to accompany her husband. This is not an unusual pattern and it further confuses children. The so-called sober parent, in attempts to maintain the relationship with the alcoholic partner and often in attempts to control the alcoholic's drinking, will drink along with the alcoholic parent and sometimes so heavily that that parent's behavior becomes as irresponsible, inconsistent and erratic as the alcoholic's behavior. "They were both absent a lot, whether there or not," is how Alicia describes the experience. The child loses both parents to alcoholism.

In the early years of Alicia's life her mother drank heavily with her father. She described her mother as a "victim," forever caught in the chaos and crisis of her husband's alcoholism, bemoaning her fate and forever focusing on events over which she had no control. While her mother always worked, her behavior alternated between being quite irresponsible when she was drinking along with her husband and then being super-responsible after the drinking episodes. As Alicia looked more closely at her own behavior as an adult, she realized that she repeats this pattern of her mother's. Although Alicia's behavior was not organized around drinking, she also alternated between being very responsible and very irresponsible.

Responsibility

This alternation between being overly responsible and irresponsible is common to people coming from a childhood of alcoholism because there are so many mixed and complicated feelings about taking responsibility. The behavior may be motivated by guilt, as Alicia's mother role-modeled when she "undid" her irresponsible drinking behavior by overdoing her responsible sober behavior. Responsibility is prematurely assumed as the result of experiences like Alicia described when her mother abdicated her role with her children and Alicia stepped in and took over. When children take on such responsibilities they believe, incorrectly, that they *should* be assuming responsibility for the behavior of others. The parents do not correct that assumption. These misconceptions may be further reinforced by that ever present and outwardly focused vision that does not allow children of alcoholism to look to themselves, and be responsible for themselves, and their own behavior. Instead they are responsible only for the behavior of others.

As they become more aware of the burdens of assuming responsibility for others, resentment grows. Relationships are regarded as burdens because they imply taking care of another's responsibilities. "I lose myself in a relationship," said one young man, and then went on to describe how being in a relationship to him means that he must negate his own needs in order to care for his partner. "The kiss of death" is how another person described the abnegation of self and one's needs that frequently is associated with being in a relationship. As a result, people often alternate between being overly involved and withdrawing completely. They will take over and try to fulfill the other's every need or refuse even to be sympathetic and compassionate, as a defense against the compulsion to take responsibility. The fear is that caring and showing interest or compassion for another will obligate them or drive them to overextend themselves and eventually lose themselves in the relationship.

Another way that being too responsible results in being irresponsible again has to do with the externalization of perception that prevents people from understanding themselves. They often are unable to recognize their own shortcomings, which necessitates their taking on more than they can accomplish and therefore

not fulfilling the commitments they make. Being too responsible
leads to being irresponsible in the end.

Alicia as the oldest daughter was in a key position to take responsibility for her family. She had an older brother who left home
when she was fourteen. But it sounded as if she had taken charge
long before her brother left home. She was twelve at the time of the
Christmas incident. Not only did she take on the responsibility for
the family's running smoothly, but she also became a leader in high
school, deriving a sense of self-worth from her school achievements. The only way she felt she could leave the family in good
conscience was by marrying at a young age. She is the only one of
the four siblings who has *not* become alcoholic. But her teenage
son became drug addicted and thus the pattern is repeating itself.

Pseudomaturity

Although Alicia is proud of her achievements as a child and
insists they made her more independent and strengthened her
character, she also points to the price she paid when she admits, "I
felt older as a kid than I do now." Alicia as a child was thrust into
adulthood, prematurely, untrained by parental role models and not
ready developmentally. Alicia's parents were too distracted by the
alcoholism to give their children's development the attention it
warranted. In a home focused around meeting the needs of the
growing children, parents teach children life skills. Complaints are
common in most families from both children and parents about
children's aversion to what behavior is acceptable in given
situations (such as eating green vegetables, practicing good table
manners or agreeing on appropriateness of clothing, makeup or
jewelry). Unpleasant as those struggles may be, they point to the
fact that families are doing their job. When parents help children
with their homework, they are usually not only teaching them
content, but also organizing and planning skills. They are
emphasizing that the school work is important and worthy of
serious attention. When a mother bakes a cake with a child, she is
teaching that child many different skills. If there is joy in the
experience, she also is teaching that there is pleasure in pro-
ductivity and in shared activities.

In families organized around alcoholism, children are often left
to learn what they can on their own. They learn haphazardly and
incompletely. They often enter adulthood with great gaps in their
knowledge of how to negotiate the practical tasks of daily living

and the social amenities and proprieties. These deficits increase the already powerful sense of insecurity and self-doubt. In some families of alcoholism, the task of educating and socializing the younger children is picked up by older siblings. This is not the same as if it were being done by the parents. The older children themselves may not have been properly taught by the parents or may not have mastered the skills they are now expected to pass on. Nor will they be motivated, the way invested parents will be motivated, to pass on their own skills, knowledge and values to the younger children. They will not have the patience that comes with maturity. The learning experience for the younger children, although better than no experience at all, will be far less satisfactory than if it were coming from an interested parent conveying to the child a delight in teaching the child, in passing on legacies and in feeling pride in the child's growing mastery. This is a tremendous loss for children who must share the parents' attention with something as compelling as alcoholism.

This is not only loss of the mastery of important life skills, but also of the experience of learning from a parent who delights in the child and the child's development. That delight adds significantly to a child's self-esteem. So does the mastery of skills. Children who are deprived of those experiences will feel anxious, fearful and inadequate to meet life's demands instead of feeling self-assured and competent. To compensate for those feelings of inadequacy and to hide them from the world and also from the self, children become caretakers.

Danny, described earlier, is the oldest of three children who had to make decisions about medical care for his parents when one of them became injured as a result of their drinking. Ill-equipped as he was to make the medical decisions he was called upon to make in childhood, but burdened as he felt, not only to care for his parents but his younger brothers as well, he wrapped himself in an aura of competence and maturity that made him credible to others. This *apparent* maturity enabled him to be effective in the areas of family life where he believed he had to take control because his parents had abdicated control. The safety of parents and siblings seemed to depend on him.

It is important to note that the concern here is about safety. Safety is translated to survival in the mind of the child. It helps to explain the intensity of the caretaking defense, the intractability of it as defense and the inability to give it up when it is no longer needed. It also explains the continuation of caretaking as a compulsion in adulthood. There is another reason for the intransigence of this defense. Caretaking makes Danny feel good. When called upon to tend to someone else or to respond to a crisis, the chronic feelings of worthlessness and inadequacy are temporarily overridden and he feels competent and adequate. The problem is not that this makes Danny feel good about himself, but that the feeling is so fleeting. This feeling will never lead to a true improvement in his self-image because it never becomes internalized; it is based on what he can do for others rather than on how he views himself. It becomes intractable because it is so gratifying and because it is one of the only ways Danny finds to feel good about himself. This very gratification prevents him from finding effective ways to increase his self-esteem.

It seems no accident that Danny chooses to work in an accident (emergency) ward. Compulsively and endlessly he repeats the medical decision making of his childhood. These attempts at achieving a sense of mastery over the work he never felt truly capable of mastering as a child do not last and so he endlessly repeats them. Unfortunately, Danny looks away to do this, attempts to achieve this sense of mastery by controlling his environment, by "fixing" others. This attempt is bound to fail because those feelings have become internalized and are no longer based on simple lack of mastery of life skills. Because they have become internalized they will not respond to external manipulations to eradicate them. Danny must look in, to himself and to those ever-present feelings of inadequacy and insecurity if he is to come to grips with the sense of inadequacy that is the result of a premature entrance into maturity.

Alicia also indicates the price she paid for her premature maturity. "I felt older as a kid than I do now," indicates some self-awareness of the awkwardness of her position, both as child and as adult. The narrowness of vision that position required of her as a child is still reflected in her behavior as adult: "I feel compelled always to have a goal," she reflects. This compulsion leaves no room for play, for relaxation or for the dropping of that "super-responsible" stance she seems to need to take at all times (unlike her mother who only assumed it after being super-irresponsible).

Many people describe this inability to play, to be childlike and to regress at appropriate times. One woman, describing her hobbies remarked, "I attack them with a vengeance. It's no fun at all. The way I play, it's work!" A young man described his first (and for a long time thereafter his last) Al-Anon ACoA meeting. "It was Christmastime and they were planning a Christmas party. They were all laughing, joking and having a good time. It made me feel awful, like I didn't belong. They weren't being serious and I couldn't understand how they could laugh and have fun. It didn't seem right. I didn't go back for two years!" Another woman, who played tennis and skied to relax became so competitive and driven to excel that she no longer enjoyed the sports she took up for enjoyment, but now feels compelled to pursue. The capacity to play, to relax, to be silly and childlike is an important asset that helps adults rejuvenate and sustain themselves and maintain a well-balanced perspective. Not having a real childhood to call forth is a real loss for the children and for the adults those children become.

This compulsion to be forever the adult reminds me of three-year-old Sally, devoted even at her age to watching over her mother — to make sure she does not use drugs. I think of Sally childlike in her pink and white striped sunsuit but on her face the worried expression of an old woman. Tiny, pale and fragile-looking, Sally's presence enlarges as she fusses over her mother, reprimands her, warns her to stop using drugs. Her situation demands a maturity beyond Sally's capabilities. Thus, she, and also Alicia and Danny and their many counterparts become pseudomature. They are forced by need (both the external needs of the situation and their own intrapsychic needs) to perform tasks and functions they are not developmentally ready to perform and for which they have no training or adequate role models. Because the children themselves are not aware that they cannot be expected to perform as adults, they feel forever ill-equipped and inadequate to perform, but see this not as consequences of the situation but of their own inadequacy.

Feelings Of Inadequacy

This sense of inadequacy is multidetermined and will be examined here only in part. Feelings of inadequacy go deep, seem immutable and influence most aspects of functioning, responses to others and self-image. Chapter 4, Part I, on caretaking described how the first goal of the child was to take care of the addiction. Three-year-old Sally felt compelled to take care of her mother's addiction. "I can make her stop using drugs," she told me, utterly convinced of the feasibility of her mission at age three. What happens when she discovers that she cannot make her mother stop using? Based on reports of older children who blame themselves for their parent's addiction, I will assume that Sally accepts this as a reflection, not of her mother's addiction but of her own inadequacy, her own lack of skill or devotion to her mother and the care of her mother.

One significant function of the illusion, the discrepancy between the way people present themselves and the way they really are, has to do with masking the sense of inadequacy from the world and sometimes even from the self. That sense of inadequacy remains untouched and uninfluenced by high achievements or praise because it is so old and goes so deep. One young man, a factory worker, illustrates this as he describes his course through high school. He never studied and wrote papers at the last minute, but still managed to pass with good grades and graduated in the top one quarter of his class. Rather than see this as an indication of an above-average intelligence, he saw it as "pulling a fast one" or just getting by without deserving to. Instead of reflecting his good natural endowment, he felt his diploma was a sign that he was a "cheat," undeserving and unworthy of his achievement. Even as he talked about this, he seemed nervous that he would lose the diploma if they ever discovered "the truth" about him. This feeling of getting by, of pulling a fast one, is a consequence of the pseudomaturity, where accomplishment never brings comfort or self-assurance because the skills it depends on are not solid, not adequately taught at the appropriate time in the child's development. As children they did get by, they did pull fast ones, because that is what they had to do. They had to attempt to do things that were realistically beyond their capacities. Instead of an internal sense of ease and a sense of capability and mastery, the inner sense is of inadequacy, a feeling of being ill-at-ease in the world. It has nothing to do with innate ability as the young laborer and a woman who participated in the same discussion both demonstrate.

As she listened to the young laborer speak, a thirty-five year old successful woman lawyer responded, "When someone praises me I think, 'If they only knew me they wouldn't say that; they'd know what a phony I am; they'd know how undeserving I am of their praise.' " Her very real achievements offer no relief from the all-pervasive sense of inadequacy. Perhaps this is because the ultimate achievement, the unadmitted but primary goal, the parents' sobriety and well-being, is never achieved and she is left therefore with an underlying and untouchable sense of failure.

Alicia's "I had so little control over so much," seems to echo this sense of inadequacy, the understanding that she was ill-equipped for the task at hand. Trying to control the uncontrollable and cope with the consequences of someone else's out-of-control behavior left her not only with a deep sense of inadequacy but also with deep fears around the issue of control: control of out-of-control parents, control of out-of-control situations as the result of out-of-control parents, control of herself and her powerful, overwhelming feelings.

Caretaking To Manage Emotion

"I never felt alone because I was taking care of my brother and sister. I never felt scared. I felt responsible." Alicia with these words points to how she deals with unmanageable feelings. Alicia paints a picture of a child who was terribly alone and also terribly afraid and angry about it. Without someone there to help her with those feelings, she had to manage them alone. Alicia had no one to teach her a healthy expression of emotion. Her parents either expressed their feelings through drunken behavior or suppressed them in sullen silence. They were too distracted by their own problems to be attentive to Alicia's feelings, to mirror or validate and label her feelings as she expressed them. When she attempted to express herself she was often cut off or reprimanded for causing trouble or being a nuisance.

Alicia learned other ways to manage those feelings. She did so by denying them, by turning away from herself and her feelings and by turning toward her role as caretaker and her sense of responsibility for her brother and sister. Alicia used caretaking to avoid her feelings. Yet those feelings persist, taking their toll on her functioning and sense of well-being. The caretaking in this case is not channeling negative feelings into something productive and acceptable. Those feelings do not get worked through but lead instead to compulsive behavior that is not self-protective or ultimately in Alicia's best interests. Alicia will have to face the negative feelings that lay beneath her caretaking if she is to get relief from the compulsiveness and nonproductivity of her caretaking.

Emma, described earlier as the mother of a young drug addict who herself has struggled with life-long suicidal urges, goes to extremes to avoid pain and conflict. In interviews with me she illustrated how she used her role as caretaker with her daughter to avoid facing other more painful feelings. When discussing her former husband or her alcoholic father, her speech quickly became disjointed and confused. As her feelings emerged, her capacity declined, as evidenced by her confusion and inability to articulate clearly. As soon as she began to talk about her daughter Jackie's finances or living arrangements, she became alert, focused and coherent. She was able to rally by suppressing her emotional pain and focusing off herself and onto problem-solving for her daughter.

Danny also uses his highly-developed caretaking skills to manage what might seem otherwise like unmanageable feelings. To avoid his own sense of helplessness, the helplessness of a young child forced to care for drunk and injured parents when he was clearly not equipped to do so, he replays those childhood scenes as an adult, when he *is* equipped to manage medical emergencies. His competence as an adult does not reassure him, does not eliminate the need to repeat the old scenes. The helplessness he repeatedly overcomes in the emergency room is not the helplessness of a skilled young doctor about to call on his newly learned skills. It is instead the unrecognized, unacknowledged helplessness of the young child repeatedly called on by sick or injured parents to take care of them or to be an adult when he is still just a child. Danny feels competent, in control and not helpless as he functions in the emergency room, and this is positive reinforcement to continue what he is doing. But the feelings of competence never last, do not get internalized and therefore he must keep rescuing and saving others. Doing this also enables him to "look away" from the other deeper feelings that might threaten to emerge were he not to keep them away with his current caretaking. Instead of freely choosing his profession, Danny is driven by the need to avoid feelings he suspects are unmanageable.

Crisis Living

Crisis living is a product of alcoholism that not only involves the alcoholics but also those who live with them. It is a life organized around the crises that inevitably result from alcoholic behavior rather than a life organized around the healthy needs of the family. Even after they have left home and established lives that are not controlled by an alcoholic, adults from such a childhood may find themselves still living from crisis to crisis. For crisis living may be another way to manage emotion. Danny, as he works in a hospital emergency room, continuously relives the medical emergencies he experienced as child with his alcoholic parents. This crisis living repeats childhood patterns and probably feels familiar if not satisfying. Crisis living in this instance is an attempt to achieve a sense of mastery, a sense of control over those helpless and out-of-control feelings of childhood.

Again, the problem is not that Danny receives a good feeling from the experience, but that the feeling is not enduring because the behavior does not in any way increase his self-esteem. This behavior can be seen as very similar to an alcoholic's drinking: behavior that is used to avoid negative feelings but that does nothing to work on the source of those feelings. Danny corroborates this as he reports that the emergencies he is regularly called on to treat evoke feelings of intoxication, "like getting high." Others report that when the alcoholic they live with stops drinking and the crises subside, life becomes "boring" and they feel dissatisfied with relationships that do not call on them to be forever rescuing their loved one. Although being dependent on the presence of crises to manage difficult feelings seems like a solution, it becomes a further problem because it forces Danny to be always living in a state of crisis. At the same time it prevents him from working on the insecurities that generate those feelings.

Alicia reports that she lives "from crisis to crisis." To constantly focus on crisis, which is external, allows her to avoid looking at herself and her own feelings. Although this may seem to protect her from her own unacceptable emotions, those feelings take their toll on her by compelling her to stay in a state of crisis. Those unrecognized feelings also make her feel forever the victim, her life forever controlled from without by others and by situations over which she has no control. Her perspective therefore recreates the role of the victim that she was in reality as a child, but need not be as adult. Were she to perceive things differently, she would be able to focus on herself and the realistic controls she does have over her own life. This perception is further reinforced by her image of her mother. Although she disdainfully describes her mother as a victim and clearly struggles against this image for herself, she also repeats it. She has incorporated it as an integral but despised part of her own identity.

Crisis living may also provide the same kind of gratification that Alicia achieved by being a leader in high school. Always solving other people's problems, resolving crises around her can make her feel competent and valued. This feeling about herself is only there in relation to caring for others. Because her self-esteem was not fostered by a consistently loving, attentive and nurturing environment from a very early age, it has not been internalized and is therefore dependent on the valuation of others. Her self-esteem is thus a fragile phenomena and she needs constant reminders that she is okay. Her self-image may require the equivalent of ongoing, chronic crisis to provide her with that sense that she is okay.

Crisis living may also help give Alicia a sense of identity. If Alicia's mission in life is to take care of others, particularly her parents, she then measures herself and even identifies herself only in relation to that mission. "Identity? What identity? I was so busy taking care of everybody else that I lost myself in the process," said one middle-aged woman describing just such an experience. A young man, also looking at his experiences caring for others said, "You talk of finding my identity as if I'd lost it. I don't think I ever had one. It is all related to others and how they think about me." Resolving crises that come always from without justifies Alicia's existence as an adult, just as taking care of her family justifies her existence as a little girl. Alicia's crisis living, coupled with her compulsive need to keep always focused on a goal, may provide her with an identity. This identity, the only one she knows, is based on the sense of herself as it relates to others, to taking care of others and to solving problems for others.

Control

Focusing on what she can do gives her a sense of control to counter the feelings of being out of control. This becomes a life-long pattern. Alicia reports that in her failed marriage and subsequent relationships control becomes a central issue. She finds herself being either too controlling or, in attempts to prevent that, becoming too submissive with her partners. The issue of control also leads her to focus on the weaknesses and inadequacies of others so that she can always be prepared to rescue them. Feeling the need to be in control she cannot see other people's ability to control their own lives and deal adequately with their own problems. She sees those she is close to as helpless and out-of-control (as were her parents) and herself as having to control them.

"I had so little control over so much," Alicia says with sadness in her voice and the helplessness of a young child trying to do far more than one should expect a child to do. When I ask her to elaborate on what she means by "so little control over so much" she vaguely answers, "emotions, the family situation," and then her voice trails off. But those are telling words. They highlight significant issues. Emotions *are* frightening to a child in an alcoholic family where parental behavior is often out of control. A violent and abusive father and a sometimes drunk and sometimes sober but always victimized mother are not models to teach a child about moderation or effective expression of emotion. The child must fear that her parents will go even more out of control than they already are and that she must somehow prevent this. This prompts the child to take control. Eventually that tendency becomes a need. Once it does, that need to take control in difficult or threatening situations becomes rigid and deeply entrenched, and persists when it is no longer helpful or productive. For children of alcoholism the need to take control, which is initially an attempt to resolve problems, becomes eventually a significant problem in itself.

In addition, where does the child learn self-control when her parents are so out of control? What fears of losing control does this stimulate in the child? Alicia fears loss of control in both others and herself. Control becomes an issue both intrapsychic and interpersonal. Although she never described the particulars of it for me, she indicated continuing struggles over control. In her failed marriage, she reports unending problems with her husband who wanted to control her. She adds, "Fighting his control led to the end of the marriage." At work she found herself "too stern" with her employees and when she got into her present romantic relationship, she found herself becoming "too submissive." Alicia always describes her work and love relationships in terms of control. She never mentions qualities she likes or dislikes about the person with whom she becomes involved. She never speaks of affection, warmth or pleasure. She never speaks of need satisfaction or lack of it. She looks only at who is controlling whom and always with a view to how the *other* person structures the relationship. This is the vision of a victim who does not see her own contributions to the interactions.

One Family's Struggles With Control

Alicia is not unique in her concerns about control and their connections with caretaking. Tina is thirty-two years old. She was described in an earlier chapter at age twelve when her parents separated. She is one of three children whose mother's tranquilizer abuse and maladaptive lifestyle became increasingly worse at the time of the parents' separation. The children had to shop, cook and clean as their mother spent more and more time alone in her room "feeling sorry for herself" as Tina disdainfully describes it. In Tina's family there is a very explicit, overt battle for control. The battle is striking in the extent to which it intrudes into all of the relationships in the family and far-reaching in its impact on each of the children. In their late twenties and early thirties, these siblings are all very attractive and intelligent people, accomplished in their work lives but still struggling unsuccessfully with their problems with their mother.

Tina spoke with me first about these problems. Her first memory goes back to when she was five years old. Normally gruff, aggressive and seemingly self-assured, she drops this image for a moment. Her eyes fill with tears as she whispers, "Sometimes I think she hates me." She is speaking of her mother. She then went on to say how her mother delighted in telling people how young Tina came up with so many logical reasons why she did not need to wear a snowsuit that her mother *gave in* to her five-year-old daughter's logic and sent her to school instead in a winter jacket. According to Tina, her mother was already losing battles with a five-year-old (battles Tina feels her mother always has engaged in with her). This is a double message to Tina for her mother shows both pride in Tina's strength and resentment of her ability to win battles with her.

This pattern repeats itself still in the present. As I held family sessions with Christine (the mother) and her three children, she seemed to single out Tina frequently as the "heavy," giving Tina a control over her life that is clearly inappropriate. She then treats Tina with anger and resentment for being so "controlling." And Tina, whether as a "loyal" daughter or because the issue of control is by now so deeply ingrained, continually complies by being inappropriately controlling with her mother. Although Christine engages in similar battles with each of her children, there is a stridency in the way she attacks Tina that singles Tina out. Clearly, Christine saw Tina as powerful and in control, and herself as a helpless victim dependent on her daughter and abused by her. At the same time there is an aggressiveness in the way she attacks Tina, a spark of vengeance in her eyes that would indicate she is even in her own eyes more than a simple victim.

But it has gone beyond just the relationship with her mother, Tina sadly admits. Control, she reflects, is a problem in all of her relationships. In a humorous manner she gives what appears to be a trivial example: She was spending the week visiting her sister and finding it difficult to live even for that brief time in such close quarters with another individual. "I came in to my sister's tiny apartment and I just took over. I didn't realize it. But finally my sister accused me of taking control of her closet!" She paused for a moment and then added, "And I had!" The humor in her eyes as she told this story quickly changed to fear as she realized how little "control" she has over her own concerns about control. The story seemed less trivial when it was over than when it began.

The Varied Aspects Of Control

Each of Christine's children have stories about their problems with control in regard to their mother. And while the content of many of them may seem trivial, the intensity and discomfort that accompanies the telling of each indicates that they are anything but trivial. Perhaps because control is not the only issue. If one looks more closely, this battle for control seems to be a struggle over who takes care of whom. This struggle not only involves Tina but also her younger sister and older brother as well. Unlike many families where one child is "elected" to be caretaker to the parent, in this family each child at various times was called upon to take care of their mother's physical and emotional needs. Joe, the oldest and the only boy, took over as head of the household and mother's confidant after his father left. This did not last long as he left home soon after. Much of the responsibility then fell to Tina, the oldest daughter and her mother's namesake.

But Jane, the youngest, also assumed some of the responsibility. She became most consistently her mother's confidant, whereas Tina became most consistently her mother's sparring partner. Said Jane of her relationship with her mother, "I feel good about me when I can do something for her." This leaves her extremely vulnerable given the battles in the family over caretaking and how ambivalent an act it becomes for each of them. Christine often controls by being helpless; the children sense this but do not know how to respond to it. Wanting to take care of their mother when she is genuinely in need of help, they realize that sometimes her helplessness is a manipulation to get them to do something for her that she could just as well do for herself. They know it is in her best interests for Christine to become more autonomous and less dependent on them. However, they often feel caught, not knowing which way they are being more helpful, by helping her or making her do for herself. This situation is further complicated by the reaction Jane described when she said she feels good about herself when she is doing something for her mother. She may feel very "bad" about herself when she is *not* doing something for her mother. Her self-esteem, the very value she places on herself, becomes tied to her ability to take care of her mother. This connection of self-esteem with taking care of their mother operates with varying degrees for each of them.

When Christine finally entered inpatient treatment for her chemical dependency, her children, all adults and scattered throughout the country, rapidly and frantically began calling me, as the family therapist, to find out what to do about their mother. While the specifics of each call were different, the nature of the questions was strikingly similar. All questioned how much they should do for her and how much she should be doing for herself. I was amazed at how quickly they all rearranged their busy schedules and flew in for a series of individual and family sessions. They each seemed starved for input on how to manage the unmanageable, how to differentiate between their mother's reasonable and unreasonable demands on them and how to sort out their own very conflicted and ambivalent feelings about her. In each session with each person, the theme remained the same.

Joe was the most unemotional, the most business-like and goal directed and the most impassive until in a family session he revealed, "Sometimes it's clear that her demands on me are unreasonable or unnecessary and then it's not hard to say no to her. At other times her requests seem reasonable and it's easy to say yes." He hesitates, his impassivity crumbling as he attempts to choke back the tears evoked by his next words. "But most of the time it isn't clear. I can't be sure what's right. Then I don't know what to do. And whatever I do it doesn't feel right." He stopped, fearful it seemed of losing control over his feelings of helplessness, rage and inadequacy. He turned pale, began to tremble, clenched his hands into fists and remained tense and withdrawn for several minutes, only slowly regaining his color and composure as he listened to his sisters talking about similar dilemmas. He was gradually drawn back into the session by the compelling nature of the issues being discussed. Not knowing what to do evoked powerful feelings for Joe.

Jane picked up when her brother became upset, instinctively, it seemed to me, rescuing him from his own emotion by changing the subject. In actuality, she didn't change the subject; she just made slight changes in the cast of characters and then gave further elaboration. She described a recent example of the same dilemma Joe had just portrayed. Several months earlier Christine had called Jane saying she "needed to get away" and wanted to come visit Jane and her family. It was a bad time for Jane who had many obligations with her husband and children; so she told her mother the visit would have to wait a few months. Jane paused, as if reluctant to go on and then shuddered but plunged ahead. "Mother got very quiet, a quiet I've come to dread because it indicates that I have hurt her. When she finally responded her voice sounded cold and deeply wounded." Jane evinced horror at the thought of hurting her mother, something beyond a normal sensitivity to another's feelings. When I asked about how it felt to hurt her mother, she went on to explain that she felt like a bad daughter who had rejected her mother. This was very difficult and painful for Jane, who prides herself on her ability to be rather consistently available to her mother.

This availability it turns out, is a highly charged issue in the family, representing far more than it would appear. For to be available, all of the children agree, determines who will be in their mother's good graces at any given time. The most sympathetic or receptive child not only will experience the beneficence of their mother's acceptance, but will also then hear about how "selfish," "insensitive" or "controlling" another child is when the latter refuses to be available to Christine at a given moment. When Jane postponed her mother's visit, she quickly realized that she had fallen from her mother's grace and that she was now being perceived by her mother as the withholding, rejecting child. (It might be more accurate to describe this as Jane becoming the withholding, rejecting *mother* as roles reversed and Christine put herself in the position of needy child in regard to her own children.) Given Jane's earlier remark "I feel good about me when I can do something for her" Christine's reaction will have an intensified impact on Jane, making her feel bad about *herself* as well as about her interaction with her mother.

This is a reaction from an earlier time. If, when they were very young, Christine's love and acceptance of her children were always conditional and always based on their ability to comply with or meet her own narcissistic needs, then the children feel their own worth is also conditional. Self-esteem is then based, not on their innate worthiness as experienced by an unconditionally loving parent at a crucial time in their development, but only on their ability to meet their mother's needs. Not meeting her needs is tantamount to being unworthy and unlovable, not just as daughter or son, but as human being.

No wonder, then, that events that may seem trivial, take on such importance for each of them. One such event I call "The Battle of the Sandwich." It occurred during Christine's hospitalization and was brought up in a family session right after the event. Christine was planning her first day trip home from the hospital. She called Tina and asked her to do some marketing so that there would be food in the house for lunch. Tina, quite possibly out of her own unrecognized resentment, did not respond directly to her mother's request. Because Christine's need to take more responsibility for herself and the management of her life was a major issue under discussion in the family sessions, Christine assumed that Tina's lack of response to her request meant that she was refusing to do the marketing. Hurt and angry but unable to say so, Christine stopped at a market on the way home and bought the makings for sandwiches. She was secretly proud of herself for this act of independence, but at the same time could not keep it separated from her own feelings of being abandoned by her daughter.

The children all gathered around her table as Christine proudly spread out the food, feeling for the moment like the generous and nurturing mother that she would like to be. Tina, whether responding to her mother's new behavior or simply continuing her endless attempts to be given to by her mother, asked her mother to fix her a sandwich. Christine, her vindictiveness winning out over her desire to nurture, responded sarcastically and with triumph in her eyes, "Really Tina, you should be more independent. Fix it yourself!"

Unable to see that she had hurt her daughter, Christine was proud as she related this story, feeling for once not like a victim and that she had repaid her daughter for what she perceived as her daughter's cruel and controlling behavior. When all of the children responded angrily after Christine related this story, she was genuinely confused and hurt. She had so construed relationships as battles for caretaking and control that she has no ability to empathize with her children or to understand their need for her as a giving mother. Thus she saw her rejection of Tina's request as simply a battle won with no ability to see this as reflection of her inability to mother or of her daughter's need for a more giving mother.

The results of these kinds of repeated interactions are damaging to all of them. By making so many demands on her children, Christine leaves herself open to having many of those demands rejected. When this happens she feels both abandoned and controlled, as if they have made the decision as to whether a given demand (which she experiences as a need) is valid or not. This increases her sense of helplessness. But she also uses that helplessness to control them, getting them to do for her when she could be doing for herself and then treating them as disloyal and rejecting when they deny her. They respond by feeling unworthy, guilty and angry. These reactions then color their responses to her which take on the quality of angry rejection reinforcing Christine's belief. Christine's demands on her children and her fury and fear when they say no to her, are clearly echoes of her own childhood; her own sense of being "unfed" and inadequate motivate her manipulative behavior. For her children her behavior is cruel and the impact on them is devastating. Issues around caretaking and control blur and are surrounded by feelings of anger, rejection and worthlessness.

Caretaking As Identity

Alicia and Danny demonstrated how organizing their adult lives around crisis living gives them an identity and measure of self-esteem they cannot achieve internally. Alex, the paraplegic young man who would call the police to protect his mother from his father's drunken violence, provides a striking example of how caretaking also becomes an identity and perhaps the only justification for existence. Alex in Chapter 5 was described as behaving his feelings rather than expressing them. Drinking, daredevil acts and reckless risk taking became his way of "running away" from his feelings, of denying his feelings. With a father too ominous and erratic in his behavior and a mother too preoccupied with her alcoholic husband, Alex had no one to quell his anxieties about his own survival. Because violence was a frequent occurrence, survival was frequently on young Alex's mind. He defends himself with denial. In areas that he perceives as most vital to his survival he repeatedly arms himself with denial — denial of his emotions, denial of his alcoholism, denial of his unmet dependency needs. To survive is to deny. To deny one looks away. For Alex the results are ultimately tragic as his survival techniques lead to more and more risk taking and alcoholic drinking that drove him to several car accidents, the last of which crippled him forever.

One also can look away by becoming caretaker, so that one looks at others and not at the frightened, needy self. Alex uses this defense also. He avoids his feelings by becoming caretaker, by taking care of his mother rather than expecting her to take care of him. By focusing on his worries about her he can avoid facing his worries about himself and who will adequately and consistently take care of him. When his father got drunk and violent Alex would call the police to break up the physical fights between his mother and his father. Alex became so vigilant that he would call the police sometimes in advance of his father's arrival home, if the hour became late and Alex was worried that the lateness of the hour indicated the degree of his father's drunkenness and, therefore, the level of his violence. Alex, even at seven and eight years old, saw himself as responsible for the safety of his mother and sisters.

Once Alex became crippled, it might appear that he had given up the role as caretaker in his family. But Alex let it be clear that that role, whether directly expressed through behavior or not, had been internalized and was still a vital part of how he saw himself. This became evident during a therapy group for adult children of alcoholics that Alex attended as part of his inpatient rehabilitation for his alcoholism. He had learned, as a result of the didactic component of the group, that caretaking of others can be counterproductive. In responding to that material, Alex described a trip home he had made the weekend before. He lived at a distance from the hospital and therefore took a plane. He liked being home and found it hard to leave. When asked about that he said, "They were all there, my mother and three sisters. I knew I had to go back to the hospital. I knew I couldn't take care of them anymore." As if reluctant to go on, he paused and then decided to proceed. This time his voice devoid of all feeling he said, "When I got on the airplane and knew I was leaving them, not able to protect them anymore, I didn't care about anything. I almost didn't care if the plane crashed or not." There was another pause, even longer. "In fact," he finally continued, "I kind of wished it would crash." Alex looked down, silent.

This was the first time that Alex touched on the possibility of his own death, despite his numerous near fatal accidents, his continuing collisions with danger. It was the first time he had even hinted at having thoughts or fantasies about death. His connecting the loss of his role of caretaker with his death could have many meanings. Caretaking provides a sense of well-being, a belief that one is needed, important and valuable. It is often the only source of feeling valuable. Without that gratification and validation for one's very existence, life may not seem worth living. To give up the role of caretaker is an unbearable loss, Alex indicates as he links it to suicidal thoughts. He is not alone in this reaction.

After a long silence, someone else in the group spoke up. It was a middle-aged housewife and mother of three young children. She described a reaction similar to Alex's when she felt her caretaking role in her family was being threatened: "They told me I needed to stay longer in the hospital. I went to my room and my first thought was to do something to myself, to hurt myself." She paused, reflected and then continued, "You know, we come in here to stop drinking so we can become *better* caretakers. Then you tell us we shouldn't be. You take that away from us." She smiled bitterly, "It's so ironic!" Alex nodded, unsmiling.

Both of these stories link the loss of the caretaking role with thoughts of self-destruction. This underscores the importance of the meaning and the power of the caretaking role as defense. When Alex experienced the loss of his role as caretaker, he no longer wanted to live. He suddenly lost his justification for living; he lost the meaning he heretofore had attached to his existence. His identity until therapy had revolved around seeing himself as the caretaker for his mother and sisters. How will he organize his identity without this crucial role? How will he regard himself? The little self-esteem he had came from this role. How will he value himself without it?

Caretaking need not always be such a self-destructive, self-defeating enterprise. To be sensitive to the needs of others, to want to reach out and be helpful to others, to be charitable and altruistic can be among the finest and noblest of human endeavors. When caretaking is used as a defense, it is just the opposite. Rather than being an indication of healthy functioning, it becomes instead compulsive, driven behavior that is not helpful to anyone. Taking care of someone who could very well take care of himself is not helpful or healthy to either member of the interaction. Taking care of someone else and ignoring one's own needs is not healthy either. Taking care of others to avoid working through one's feelings of anger, helplessness or inadequacy keeps one fixated at feeling angry, helpless and inadequate. One has to learn how to take care of oneself before one can be truly helpful to another. Ironically, children of alcoholism, who become so devoted to caring for others, have rarely learned how to take care of themselves. Not until they have learned how to identify their own needs and get those needs met, to identify and express their feelings and to take responsibility for their own behavior, will they be optimally helpful to those who need and love them.

PART IV

The Future

CHAPTER 10

The Process Of Change

Why Change?

Over and over again people proudly tell me of the positive qualities they have developed as a result of growing up under the influence of parental alcoholism. They are keenly aware of their self-sufficiency and ability to function well, often superbly, under stress. These feelings of competence are often linked to the ability to endure what others might find unendurable, to make the most of what others would find unworkable and to tolerate the intolerable. The phrase, "But I survived!" is repeatedly spoken with intense pride and affirmation of the strength that survival entailed. That pride and affirmation are well-deserved. The strength, the self-sufficiency, the ability to endure should be respected and valued by those who possess those qualities and by those who work with them. They can be called on for more than survival if properly appreciated and understood.

But the very survival techniques that deserve pride and affirmation also take a toll on the survivors. It is this toll, the childhood adaptations that ultimately result in maladaptation that cry for change, that require change if the quality of life is to improve. When adaptations, coping techniques or defense mechanisms are linked in the child's mind to survival they remain fixed below the level of consciousness, rigid and not available to adaptation and change as the child develops and grows. If children fear that survival is at stake, then they do not feel comfortable experimenting with new ways to respond to situations or people. They stay instead with the known, the survival techniques that have worked for them in the past. Continuing to use adaptations from an earlier time in life, called *fixation,* means that one is left with coping mechanisms that may not be nearly as effective in responding to new, healthier and particularly to nonalcoholic situations. Unfortunately, a person who tends to see all conflicts or problems as connected to survival because of the early experiences will not risk survival to experiment or explore. It is through experimentation and exploration that growth and development occur. Adults coming from those kinds of early experiences do not have available to them more flexible or more adaptive coping mechanisms because they dared not risk acquiring them during childhood. They are therefore left with the early adaptations.

Recreating The Past

When people apply childhood adaptations to adult situations they find themselves repeating old scenes. The ways people approach and react to situations help shape them. Thus even relationships and situations that potentially have no similarity to the childhood may come to resemble the childhood. For example, the daughter who always rescued her alcoholic father may treat her husband as if he were incompetent, irrational and inadequate, because that is how the most important man in her life acted when he was drunk or hung over. Although the daughter may have purposely sought out a competent, rational and nonalcoholic husband, her automatic and unconscious perceptions will influence her experience of her husband. She may instinctively rush to rescue or do for him when he is quite capable of taking care of himself. She may be far more attuned to his weaknesses than to his strengths and with all good intentions believe that she must protect him from his weaknesses. If he is secretly insecure and worried about his own adequacy then her rescuing will reinforce that and he may come to act and eventually believe in her perceptions. He then will let her do for him and rescue him, but the relationship will have degenerated to recreate the earlier alcoholic relationship even if he is not alcoholic.

Conversely, if he is comfortable and secure in his competence he will resist (and be displeased by) her efforts to rescue and manage him. This could cause significant conflict and distress in the relationship. In addition, it will result in two possible outcomes for her. She will be left without the gratification of having someone to save. This will leave her feeling inadequate because that is where her sense of adequacy has resided. Deprived of the sense of adequacy, eventually she will become depressed. The other outcome is that she may be left feeling out of control of the situation, because he will not allow her to control him as her father did. This will increase her anxiety and feelings of helplessness. In either case, the hoped-for outcome, to live comfortably in a situation free of any resemblance to the past will not happen and in some form the past will have been re-created.

There are other reasons that people find themselves reliving or re-creating the past without intending to. One is that people tend to search out the familiar, which even though it may be unpleasant, is also the comfortable. The known, the familiar, the new scenes that resemble older scenes, allow the child of alcoholism to quite easily and even successfully use the old, proven defenses and responses. Some people are dismayed to discover they have somehow unknowingly and unintentionally surrounded themselves with alcoholics or people with other addictive disorders. Others find with equal dismay that they have become addicted to some substance or activity themselves, despite their absolute determination *not* to repeat the "sins of their fathers."

Not all people make the same adaptations with the same degree of rigidity or flexibility. The differences are determined by a number of factors, including the temperament and disposition of each child and the nature of his exposure to parental alcoholism. The degree of maladaptation may also be related to the child's age at the inception of parental alcoholism; the position of the child within the family; the sex of the child and the sex of the alcoholic parent; the duration and intensity of the alcoholism and its ability to disrupt family life; the effect of the alcoholism on the sober spouse; the duration and intensity of the child's exposure to it and the availability and influence of other role models in the child's life.

It is usually the rigidity and frequency of the use of particular defenses that determine how counterproductive or maladaptive they become. All people have their own characteristic ways of coping. The particulars of each person's repertoire will contribute to the definition of personality type, style and character. When survival is not the determining issue in the choice of coping strategies, one usually has a certain flexibility in terms of what one brings to a given situation. For example, in some situations the best way to handle a crisis is to remain calm. In those situations, suppression of feelings might be the most appropriate solution. In other crises it might be more productive to let one's feelings dictate an appropriate response. In those situations suppression of feelings will be a hindrance. To be able to call forth the most productive response in a given situation is optimal. To be able to do this requires a flexibility and comfort with various ways of coping. One might have preferences and typical responses, but one should also have the flexibility to make other choices when the situation so indicates. If someone has learned at an early age that the only way to survive threatening situations is to suppress feelings and if that person also experiences all threatening situations as connected to survival, then that person will lose the flexibility of response. Each situation that provokes threat will be responded to in automatic, unquestioning and rigid ways — by the suppression of feeling. The perceived connection to survival rigidifies the response and it is the rigidity of the response that determines how productive or maladaptive it is in a given situation.

The Power Of The Unconscious

The apparent success of certain adaptations in childhood ensures they will continue to be used. In adulthood, they will emerge automatically whenever circumstances evoke the childhood feelings. This means that the adult is left with a child's repertoire of reactions to deal with trauma or the threat of trauma. For many children of alcoholism threats to their well-being were frequent and unpredictable, dependent not on the child and the child's feelings or behavior but on unreliable and unpredictable adults. Because these threats often were of great significance (compromising physical or emotional security), the child was always alert for possible trouble. This supersensitivity to impending trouble, which is adaptive in childhood, becomes an overreaction in adulthood. The sense of impending doom, real or not, persists and calls forth the old responses even though the situations are not similar. What is similar, and what calls forth their use is the old feelings that have been evoked. This is what is meant by the unconscious influence of the past on present behavior. When these solutions are unconscious, they are not subject to objective scrutiny nor used purposefully and appropriately. They are used instead instinctively and automatically whenever old feelings threaten to emerge.

As these solutions are called on in new and different situations their use helps reshape those new situations into resembling the old ones that the children have been so determined to escape. Billy provides an example of behavior that remains unquestioned. Billy was the child who would put his head under the covers so as not to hear his alcoholic mother threaten suicide when she fought with Billy's father. Without realizing it, he recreates in adulthood his childhood experiences in only slightly altered form. We can speculate on why he does this: to achieve a sense of mastery over a life that feels very much "unmastered;" to ultimately control the uncontrollable; to avoid becoming aware of feelings of anxiety or inadequacy; these may all be part of what motivates him. But the fact that this is unconsciously motivated behavior means that it is not in Billy's conscious control.

Early in his life Billy took on the role of protector of his mother. He would try to prevent arguments between his parents by taking on many of his mother's household responsibilities and by regularly covering up for or making excuses to his father for his mother's behavior. There were many times, however, when Billy was unable to prevent the fights or the drunken driving that was often an after-effect of such arguments. Billy would then cope by running up to his room and burrowing himself under his blankets to block out the sounds of the arguing and his mother's suicide threats or the slamming of the front door and the starting up of the car in the middle of the night. When all else failed, blocking out painful scenes and conflict became a way of surviving for Billy. He also became adept at blocking out his own pain, his fear and anxiety, his desire for a nurturing and stable environment, and his anger at parents so inattentive and unprotective. Such feelings would have served him poorly when he felt his survival depended on the survival of those very fragile caretakers. In those instances, Billy blocked awareness of the pain coming from his unmet needs as a form of survival.

Billy's hyperalertness to the fragility of his parents and his ability to prevent or predict impending crises, the tact and diplomacy he developed as mediator in their marital battles as well as the ability to endure chaos, crises and hardship have all served Billy well as an adult. He became a highly successful businessman, a loyal and devoted husband and father. But he also found himself repeating the very patterns he was absolutely determined to avoid. He so successfully blocked awareness of the things over which he felt most powerless that, despite his conscious determination never to marry a woman like his mother, he did just that. He did this at least in part by never perceiving the potential problems with her heavy drinking and by blinding himself to her frequent pill taking and erratic mood swings. Instead he focused on how delightful and loving she was when sober, refusing to notice her increasing alcohol and drug use and minimizing her suicidal tendencies.

Billy had learned to create blind spots for himself when his anxiety around his mother's alcoholic and self-destructive behavior became intolerable. Unable to control her behavior, he learned to pull the covers over his head when possible and to put on emotional and even intellectual blinders when he could not physically block out the anxiety-provoking events. For Billy, blinders became the route to emotional survival and to controlling what might otherwise be overwhelming, uncontrollable feelings. This worked for him as a child. Unable to make his mother stop drinking, stop taking too many pills or stop driving when intoxicated, he protected himself from the fear of losing her by not hearing, not seeing and not understanding the implications of her behavior. Although this may have been the most adaptive way to deal with the feelings his mother evoked in him by her irrational, alcoholic behavior, it does not serve him well in adulthood and does not prevent him from repeating old, unwanted scenes from his past.

Billy focused as a child not on the amount of his mother's drinking, over which he had no control, but on repairing the damage (when he could) done by her drinking. The same thing occurred when he met his wife. He did not recognize that she was a heavy (potentially problematic) drinker, which might have discouraged him from becoming interested in her given his conscious determination not to marry an alcoholic. This is surprising, considering his sensitivity to alcoholism. This gap in his perception makes little sense rationally. It points to the fact that something not obvious, not under Billy's conscious control may be operating. Although the blindness spares him anxiety or other strong negative feelings about this woman, it also enables him to marry her without taking into consideration her resemblances to his mother. But even if the reader is skeptical about the unconscious motivations at work here and insists that "love" blinded Billy to all but his future wife's good qualities, the blindness persists as the honeymoon ends and a less idealized reality takes over.

At any stage in the progression of her illness, Billy could have had significant input into his wife's behavior. As her drinking and pill taking increased, so did her complaints about her life and marriage. He ignored her. At one point she told him she thought they needed help with their failing marriage and suggested they go to a marriage counselor. He refused, claiming that she was exaggerating the severity of the problems, and insisting that if she just drank a little less they could handle their problems themselves. He bought her a new television set. She continued to drink, take pills and complain. He continued not to hear her.

Billy is responding instinctively to old fears. In the past, when his mother began to drink he would feel helpless and fearful anticipating what was to come. With no satisfactory outlet for those feelings, Billy would block them out. He reacts in similar ways with his wife, where it is no longer appropriate. When his wife begins to drink, Billy automatically responds with feelings of helplessness that he immediately blocks out by blinding himself to both her activity and his feeling. In this situation Billy need not be helpless. Had he noticed his wife's increased drinking and tranquilizer abuse, he could have helped her to get help for her chemical dependency and depression. Had he recognized his own pain and his own disappointment with the marriage, this too might have mobilized him to look for the source of the problem and then to work toward healthier solutions. Instead he reacts as if he were still that helpless, powerless little boy, and in a sense by his lack of action, he again becomes that helpless, powerless little boy. With his old, automatic response he helps to re-create the scene he dreads most.

His wife had become increasingly depressed and was not taking care of herself, the children or the house. Rather than repeat the arguments he remembered his parents having over those same issues, Billy tried instead to ignore or compensate for his wife's decreasing functioning. He began to cover up for her just as he had for his mother, picking up as many of the household responsibilities as his busy schedule would allow, making excuses for her to the children when they complained about her negligence and minimizing to himself the seriousness of her decline. Ironically, his very attempts to cope with her alcoholism allowed it to continue. His covering up for her spared her from having to face the consequences of her drinking and drinking-related behavior. Billy's response is so common in alcoholic families that a term has been coined for the role Billy plays. He is called an *enabler* because his behavior enabled her alcoholism to continue unconfronted.

Even when she started making veiled references to suicide, he did not attend to her seriously. When she began to show an interest in his gun collection, he ignored this too. Finally, after a particularly bitter tirade that Billy quietly endured, his wife took one of the guns from his collection and, accusing him of not caring whether she lived or died, put the gun to her head and pulled the trigger. Fortunately, the gun did not fire and Billy finally mobilized enough to grab the gun from her.

This incident should never have occurred. Billy, the eternal caretaker, the mollifier and pacifier of everyone's distress and the devoted husband and father, was unable to prevent this situation. He was blind and deaf to his wife's repeated distress and was negligent and irresponsible when her very life was at stake. Instead of helping Billy survive in this instance, his survival techniques plunged him back into his past, allowed his wife's addiction and accompanying depression to become so far advanced that she nearly committed suicide.

While Billy took the gun away from his wife and made sure she was safely in bed that night, still he did not take action to get her help. Nor did he remove the guns from the house. Several weeks later his wife again fired the gun. This was the second time in less than two months that a near-tragic incident was just barely averted. In neither case was it averted because Billy took appropriate action. He instead took that helpless, avoidant position of his childhood and never recognized his potential to take positive action.

When asked why he did not seek treatment for her at the time of the first incident with the gun, Billy dismissed the incident as an accident that he attributed to his wife "just having a little too much to drink." This seems highly irresponsible behavior for someone who is not normally irresponsible and for someone who loves his wife and prides himself on his ability to care for her. What does this behavior indicate? Is it denial? Is it repressed rage? Billy had no awareness at that time of any negative feelings about his wife. Yet his behavior indicates the presence of significant ambivalence or he would not have been so unresponsive to her pain and her self-destructiveness. His lack of appropriate response could be reflecting the presence of many feelings that we can only speculate about given Billy's lack of awareness. What is not speculation is that this behavior, going as it does against all that Billy consciously desires and experiences, indicates the presence of unconscious forces motivating his action. It also illustrates how such forces will dictate behavior that creates just the situations he wants to avoid. Billy was in large part responsible for the second gun incident just because he did not take action to prevent it. He re-creates, unwittingly, the very scene he believes he wants most to avoid.

That same blindness and unconsciously destructive behavior persisted even after he became more intellectually self-aware. When his wife was finally admitted to an alcoholism treatment program Billy, as part of the family program, began to get help for himself. This help included education and therapy. Slowly he began to examine what had previously been unexamined: his behavior. As he began to read some of the literature on adult children of alcoholics, he began to recognize some of his patterns, particularly his tendency to pacify others and to avoid conflict. He began to think that perhaps marrying a wife who became alcoholic might not be the accident he had thought it was. He began to attribute his lack of confrontation of his wife's alcoholism to his desire to avoid conflict. He began to see some of the rationalizations he made about her drinking, drug taking and depression as ways to avoid dealing with situations that he felt incapable of handling. While these are only beginning insights into the nature of a very complex set of behaviors and motivations, still they represent a significant change for Billy in that he finally began to explore what until then seemed to be familiar terrain.

As Billy began this slow examination of his life and behavior, still he kept the gun collection in his house, and this despite his wife's continued depression and occasional relapses of drinking. He insisted at first that she would not make another suicide attempt. After persistent confrontation and after many weeks had passed, he finally hid the guns in the attic of the house. He absolutely refused to acknowledge that she could find them if she were determined to do so. Each time the guns were brought up, he became suddenly, automatically and adamantly blind and unable to see how this might be inappropriate behavior even when directly confronted with the idea.

This irrational behavior of Billy's is again indication that something unconscious is occurring. Billy's air of unconcern, his lack of anxiety around the guns remaining in the house and his adamant refusal to even look at his decision, is striking. This blindness, this lack of anxiety actually becomes dangerous, leads Billy to not protect the one he most cares about and perpetuates the very same kinds of scenes that he grew up with and had been so determined to avoid. This blindness cannot be dismissed as accidental, a onetime oversight by a distraught and overworked husband. This blindness recurred repeatedly at each phase of the progression of her illness. And at each phase steps could have been taken that might have prevented further progression. Near tragedy could have been averted at each step if Billy could have felt his feelings and his ambivalence, and could have recognized his wife's alcoholism and emotional distress.

This blindness also reinforces the sense of confusion and helplessness when events recur and Billy cannot see his contribution to them. Then another old childhood feeling emerges, the feeling that he is a victim. As a child he *was* a victim. But in his marriage he is not a victim. He could have prevented his wife's near suicide had his own response to her been different. He continues to feel like a victim because he is unable to see his own contribution to the situation.

It should be remembered that the blocking out of feeling and awareness of conflict-ridden or potentially dangerous situations are Billy's attempts to resolve internal feelings of helplessness, anxiety and other overwhelming emotions. Repeatedly we have seen how this blindness does not resolve problems external or internal. Change can only occur when Billy turns his gaze inward, away from the events of his life and toward the inner life that helps shape those events. There can be no lasting, genuine change until this automatic, unexamined behavior and the unconscious reactions that motivate it become open to examination and modification. Billy cannot expect to do this alone. The very nature of the blindness imposed by unconscious forces, will dictate the need for trained, objective eyes to help him to discover what part of his behavior is unconsciously driven and therefore out of his conscious, adult control.

The Limitation Of Intellectual Understanding

Billy, determined and highly motivated to change his life by use of extensive reading materials and regular participation in a self-help group, in the early stages of therapy kept a gun collection in a house with a potentially suicidal wife. His behavior demonstrates how deep is the response to the parental alcoholism and how old responses, because they are unconsciously linked to survival, become automatic, unquestioned and entrenched. Nevertheless, it is important to remember that Billy's early solutions, maladaptive as they now are, also indicate a source of strength, tenacity and resourcefulness that not only continue to serve him well in certain situations but that also can lead him away from his current lifestyle if they are properly understood and redirected. This does not happen by chance or by desire and determination alone.

Even intellectual understanding will not lead to responding differently in situations that evoke old and deep responses. A general understanding of the patterns will not enable Billy, for example, to take off the blinders when anxiety calls them forth. And if he "sees" the behavior he may not be able to recognize it as inappropriate because his feelings influence his perceptions. And if he "sees" the inappropriateness of the behavior, he may still continue to compulsively and unhappily repeat it. This is not to say that change cannot occur, but rather to emphasize that it will take more than an intellectual understanding to bring about change. People who recognize self-destructive or maladaptive patterns but find they continue to repeat them, should not berate themselves for their failure to change. This repetitive behavior is not a sign of inadequacy or a deficiency of willpower but rather an indication of the strength of the unconscious forces operating. Other ways to work on the undesirable behavior should be explored at that point with a professional.

The answer to the initial question of this chapter, "Why change?" can be seen clearly with Billy whose use of old solutions to new problems contributed to the progression of his wife's addiction and depression. However, Billy represents only one category of response to parental alcoholism. Some adult children of alcoholics experience serious difficulties of their own, such as addiction, debilitating depression or other problematic behaviors that obviously require intervention. There are others who seem to survive unaffected by the experience and for whom no change is indicated. For others successful survival can mask difficulties that will significantly affect the quality of their lives.

Some people, while having none of the obvious difficulties described here in their relationships or in their work lives, may still experience the unconscious influences illustrated by Billy, but to a lesser degree. They may also benefit from reworking those old solutions. This is not a sign of failure, of being wrong or inadequate or weak as children of alcoholism are so quick to assume. People can consider making significant changes in their lives, not because they would not otherwise survive, but rather to improve the quality of their lives and to give them a better sense of control. Gaining a better appreciation of how the past influences the present frees people from the maladaptive influence of that past and enables current choices to be more in keeping with what they consciously want for themselves. If this is the case, then change becomes an option to be seriously considered. However change and the nature of that change pose additional problems for children of alcoholism.

Options For Change

Deciding if one wants to change and what changes are in order is always an individual choice. It is important to remember this because children of alcoholism are used to living by the dictates of others. This tendency often makes them feel like victims, driven to certain choices by circumstance rather than by a conscious, willful act. Yet the decision to embark on a process of change should be, *must* be a personal one and motivated from within if genuine change is to occur. If a person is only changing because "My husband says I need help," or "My wife is threatening to leave me if I don't do something," or "My son is in trouble and they say *I* have to change," he or she is simply repeating childhood behavior. This is still the position of a victim who does not look inward but sees the problem as existing in the environment and not in the self.

And yet the problem *is* in the self, in the way one has learned to respond to one's environment. As with Billy, even when the environment changes, he will continue to respond in the old ways unless he begins to understand himself differently and more thoroughly. In addition, again like Billy, a person may continue to gravitate toward situations that resemble the past. So the first decision a person makes regarding change, will also be the first change if it is honestly made, for it will acknowledge an acceptance of the possibility for personal choice, dependent ultimately on the self and one's needs and not on dictates from the environment.

What one changes is also a personal, individual choice. Some of the issues described in this book may not be experienced by everyone as problems or may be areas a person is unwilling to address. Again this is a personal, individual choice and should be determined by one's own level of comfort or discomfort with how things are and not by someone else's judgment or preference. One can use others to help one recognize and define problem areas, but the decision regarding what one will work on should again be very personal, individualized and one's own.

Illustrations

The first three sections of this book elaborated on some of the major problem areas for adult children of alcoholics. Here we will be concerned with a brief recapitulation of a few key issues to illustrate how they relate to the process of change.

Denial

The extensive use of defense mechanisms such as denial, minimization, rationalization and avoidance often create rather than resolve problems, preventing accurate appraisals of past and present situations and forcing people to stay in unhealthy positions that compromise their well-being. The extensive use of these defenses may also prevent people from recognizing they have a problem and therefore making the decision to get help.

Feelings

The management of emotion — knowing what they are feeling, being able to name feelings, being able to experience feelings without feeling out of control or overwhelmed, being able to use feelings constructively and as motivation for appropriate behavior — these are all potential problem areas for people who did not have help with this as children. The anticipation of having to go back over painful memories may prevent people from getting help or quickly drive them away from proper help when feelings emerge before they feel ready to handle them.

Communication

When speech has lost its integrity, when words are perceived and used only as vehicles of deception and cover-up, which happens consistently in families of alcoholism, then little real communication can occur. This increases already powerful feelings of being different, misunderstood and isolated. Not trusting what others say leaves people unable to benefit from the feedback of others to correct or be aware of the inevitable misconceptions and misperceptions that surround the experience of a childhood of alcoholism. The lack of belief in the integrity of speech can also prevent them from asking for help or from being able to use it constructively.

Caretaking

The overuse of caretaking results in neglect of the self, in remaining either unaware of needs or reluctant or unable to get them met. The compulsive need to be a caretaker results in being surrounded too often by needy, demanding people and to being too often thrust into crisis and chaos. When caretaking is used as a defense against the awareness of one's own sense of helplessness and inadequacy, it may increase the sense of competency over the short run but prevents resolving the deeper sources of that sense of inadequacy. The need to be forever the caretaker implies also that it is extremely difficult to take help from someone else or to trust another person to be consistently there and helpful.

Memory

Events remembered through the distortions of the alcoholism should be reexamined because such distortions of memory change the history of people, and relearning what in fact happened and attaching new meanings to old events can have tremendous implications regarding how people look at their lives and how they regard themselves.

Self-Esteem

Feelings of inadequacy, poor self-worth, guilt and shame impinge on the quality of life and exert control over behavior in powerful ways. People may even feel that they are incapable of change or unworthy of the efforts they must make to achieve it.

The Illusion

That deceptive presentation that children of alcoholism make to the world and often to themselves results in ongoing feelings of emptiness, of not knowing who they really are and of not really owning or being in control of their lives. The need to maintain the illusion may also keep them from admitting they need to change and as a result they live forever with the emptiness and loss of self the maintenance of the illusion creates.

How To Affect Change

The process of change can only begin when there is an understanding of what can change. As long as people expect to change their environment, which will be the tendency, the kinds of changes we are talking about here cannot occur. Manipulation of the environment and of the significant others in the environment, which adult children of alcoholics already may be quite proficient at doing, usually brings little more than temporary triumph or relief. The tendency will be to keep putting themselves in the same old binds, the same intolerable or at least extremely stressful positions, as did Billy. For change to be deep and lasting it must come from within. People must struggle with the fear, anxiety, sadness and other pain that have been the impetus for the development of the nonproductive solutions so far employed and that perpetuate rather than resolve the pain.

Internalizing Change

Therefore, the first step in the process is to recognize that change will be of the self and come from the self. It is important to remember that children of alcoholism will automatically expect not only that the problem be external but that the solution will also be external, coming from without rather than within. But, this is not the case. Just as the object of change must be the self, so too the source of change will ultimately be the self. One may develop tools and learn from others, but the ultimate solutions are within the individual and can be found only by the individual. Although people need help from others to engage in this process, they are still ultimately responsible for the process and its success or failure.

Understanding The Problem

The second step in this process will be to understand what the problems are. Utilizing a variety of resources to gain this understanding can be quite useful given the complexity of its nature. It might be helpful here to describe some of these resources for those who have no familiarity with them. Self-help groups are probably the most prevalent and visible resources today.

Self-Help Groups

Alcoholics Anonymous (AA) is the largest and best known self-help group. It is based on a 12-Step recovery program whose wisdom and applicability have led to its being adopted by other self-help groups, including Al-Anon, which is the self-help group concerned with the family members of the alcoholic. There are also self-help groups for other addictions such as drugs, food and gambling. Some of these also have groups for relatives. Those groups that have a 12-Step program provide the structure that has proven to be so successful in helping the alcoholic.

Educational Experiences Available

One other resource today is the plethora of educational experiences being provided for adult children of alcoholism. Conferences, lectures, workshops, magazine and journal articles and books provide information about the problems encountered by this population. Each of these resources has something of value to offer. No one of them alone will probably be sufficient to make the kinds of changes here described. Understanding what each can and cannot do for a given problem will help one make an informed choice about how to put together the most effective program of change for a given individual.

Reading and attending lectures and workshops are good ways to begin to get an intellectual grasp of the nature of the problem. Self-help groups (such as Al-Anon) based on the 12 Steps will increase one's understanding of the nature of co-dependency as well as appropriate and inappropriate positions to take with the alcoholic. Adult children of alcoholics (ACoA) self-help groups and short-term, structured therapy groups also will increase one's understanding of the nature of the problem. In addition, short-term therapy groups and self-help groups specifically for this group will provide much needed validation and support as one embarks on this ultimately rewarding but initially stressful process.

Psychoeducational Groups

Another growing resource is psychoeducational groups for adult children of alcoholics. These are groups whose goal is to increase awareness of this phenomenon and whose therapeutic value is based on information-giving, emotional ventilation and increased understanding. Such groups are usually short-term (several weeks to several months) and the leaders of these groups may take a very active role in determining the direction the group will take. Such groups may include a didactic component and structured activities such as role-playing. The emphasis in such groups is on behavior change, not character change.

Therapy

Short-term individual therapy may follow the same model and goals as psychoeducational groups. Long-term, unstructured individual and group psychotherapy is usually more concerned with internal or character change. These modalities of treatment will be directed toward self-discovery and self-examination and less interested in imparting didactic information or using structured activities to promote emotional or intellectual understanding. The premise here is that lasting behavior change will come as internal change occurs, that the lessening of the need for (and therefore use of) the nonproductive defense mechanisms will allow the person to function more productively and more consistently in line with what he or she consciously desires.

Long-Term Psychotherapy

Once people have some idea of what they want to change about themselves, then they must come to some understanding of how to go about making those changes. Intellectual understanding is rarely enough to enable people to make the changes they desire. Even insight, the combination of intellectual and emotional understanding, which is the beginning of true internal change, will not in itself automatically cause change. "Working through," the repeated working and reworking of important experiences over time and with continuing applications to one's life, is part of a complex, multifaceted process that will lead to change that is neither superficial nor short-lived. This process also includes the impact of the relationship with the therapist and the reworking of the traumatic past in the confines of a safe, therapeutic environment that allows more for growth and the development of healthier reactions and responses than were possible at an earlier time. To gain insight and then to work through the material derived from the insight require long-term psychotherapy. This solution is one that many adult children of alcoholics will not like to hear. They will insist that their own determination and perseverance should suffice. They will resist the discomforts that such a solution will entail. But that makes the reality no less real. The problems described here did not appear overnight nor will they go away overnight. Short-lived solutions usually bring short-lived results.

This is not to minimize the benefits of short-term therapy and self-help groups, lectures and books, but to put them in an appropriate perspective. They are important first steps on a journey of change because they offer two essential prerequisites for change for children of alcoholism: support and validation. Change of this nature is too stressful, too confusing to be initiated without support.

Validation may be the most therapeutic experience in the beginning of this process. The acknowledgment by another that what is being said is true and sound counters the denial, deception and distortions of the childhood. Validation liberates, illuminates and gives permission to go further. More about this will be discussed in the chapter on therapy, but it is so important to the process of change that it is worthy of special note at this point. Children of alcoholism know this. They appreciate the power and healing capacities of validation. Therapists and significant others, who are not sensitive to the impact of alcoholism on a child's life, may not appreciate the importance and value of validation.

Twelve-Step self-help programs and short-term therapy may also provide the foundation for a different kind of awareness of one's situation. New perceptions of old problems can lead to experimenting with new ways to problem solve which may lead to the beginnings of desired behavior changes. These resources also serve as important and sometimes essential adjuncts to and supports for the intensive internal work that can only take place in psychotherapy.

Illustrations Of How To Affect Change

Denial

There are many ways to decrease the overuse of denial and other defense mechanisms such as minimization, rationalization and avoidance. An intellectual understanding that comes through reading and workshops will begin to rework the impact of the *parents'* denial of the alcoholism on the child. Hearing behavior described and then labeled as alcoholic, which the parents never did, will help to decrease the confusion that results from living with the parents' distorted definitions (rationalization and minimization) of the alcoholic behavior. In self-help and therapy groups, hearing other people's stories cuts through the rationalizations regarding the parents' unacceptable behavior. In addition, listening to the stories of others challenges the minimizations of the parents in relation to the impact of the alcoholism on the child. And finally, as those stories evoke old and painful memories, the avoidance that was a response to those events decreases.

Feelings

Most children of alcoholism hope that reading and other solitary activities will help them in the management of their emotions. Unfortunately, this is not the case. One cannot learn by oneself to express feelings when one has never learned how to identify them. No book, conference or videotape can teach one how to express emotion. One can learn from such sources that one has a range of feelings, that feelings are neither right nor wrong, but until this knowledge is practiced with a reliable other, it is only academic. One cannot learn by oneself how to express feelings when one has never had someone to role model their appropriate expression. One cannot learn by oneself how to manage feelings when all one has seen is stoic suppression or violent acting out.

Self-help groups, with their focus on feelings and on the telling of stories, can help individuals to begin to feel and to get needed validation for having feelings. They can also provide much needed support as people begin to experience their emotions. Because the experiencing of feelings is so difficult for children of alcoholism, they often experience further trauma instead of relief when emotions start to emerge. If they are not receiving additional help and feel overwhelmed as the emotions emerge, the danger is that the emerging feelings becomes a repetitive traumatization of the old, painful experiences without the opportunity to master these traumas. Without professional help, the tendency will be to reach for old solutions. They will look for familiar ways to control the emerging pain.

One old and trusted way will be to suppress it. Another may be unwittingly offered by the very groups that are attempting to help people come to more effective solutions. Many groups use sayings and directives to help ease the discomfort and to help point the way toward more constructive responses. Unfortunately, the use of these sayings as directives may provide a way of sealing off feelings and increasing defenses. The repetitive use of sayings meant to comfort may instead help children of alcoholism to avoid the very pain they must face and learn to manage.

If, on the other hand, in attempts to respond differently, people opt not to seal themselves off from their pain, they may instead reexperience over and over traumatization from the emerging feelings. This is like opening an old wound time after time without applying proper medication to treat the wound. This does not heal the wound and in fact can make it worse. The repeated reexperiencing of trauma without professional guidance can lead to feelings of instability and regression or to once again sealing off the old pain without having worked through or resolved the problems that it uncovered. Ultimately people wonder why they are not feeling better since they are now experiencing feelings. But there will be no one to ask this question of and so they will answer with their usual response when something goes wrong, "There must be something wrong with me." In fact, there is nothing wrong with them; they simply have not put themselves in a position where they can make the kinds of changes they need to make. Tragically, rather than understanding this and seeing it as an example of incomplete problem solving, the experience instead becomes one of self-blame and failure, further reinforcing their already poor self-image. It also leaves them once again with that old message that expression of feelings is damaging and cannot be helpful or lead to new and better solutions to old problems.

Communication

Solitary experiences will not help to improve communication skills. Self-help groups and therapy can be the arena to begin to explore the value and meaning of honest communication. For the ultimate communication however, that final understanding of the deeper issues relating to one's identity and feelings about oneself, self-help groups and structured, short-term therapy groups will prove inadequate. Lists of characteristics of adult children of alcoholics, guidelines to change, structured exercises and sayings that impose rather than help reveal a personal philosophy will not in themselves lead one toward the true self but toward other people's versions of the self. True self-understanding can only come through a quiet, personal, individualized exploration. Others can only support, validate, point out the distortions in perception and interpret the use of defenses that keep one away from a true self-understanding.

Caretaking

In order to decrease the *maladaptive* use of caretaking and increase the ability to take better care of themselves, people can use a variety of modes. It is best to start by understanding the nature of the use of caretaking as defense or survival technique. This can be done in a variety of ways, through acquiring an intellectual understanding and eventually an emotional understanding of the process. Reading, conferences, self-help groups and therapy all can lead to an increased understanding of the process. The supportiveness of self-help groups can be a particularly important experience in taking better care of oneself, by the very act of attendance and the acceptance of the support of the group. These groups will also help in pointing out ways that their members are not taking care of themselves or rushing in too quickly to take care of their loved ones. In this way they provide a significant avenue to important behavioral change. And finally, going to meetings is a message to the self that one is in need of the support of others and that it is acceptable, even desirable, to take such support.

To address the underlying motives for the caretaking, to understand how this operates as defense and as such prevents growth and gives only the illusion of well-being will require an individualized approach that can only occur in therapy groups or individual therapy.

Memory

The distortions in memory that prevent a true understanding of the past and its influence on the present can best be revealed through the recognition of other people's stories as similar to one's own. This can be accomplished through reading or talking to others with similar histories and sharing stories. Often someone else's story will revive buried memories or help to put old memories in a new context that changes either their meaning or the implications that have been drawn from them.

Self-Esteem

The increase of self-esteem, if it is to be genuine, is a gradual and incremental process that will benefit from many and varied inputs. All of the previously described methods can work toward increasing one's self esteem if properly used. One must be careful, however, because these methods can all be used to decrease self-esteem also. This may not be readily apparent either to the person or to those around the person (fellow group members, therapists, loved ones). An ongoing awareness and dialogue are essential concerning the essential assaults to self-esteem if attempts at change are not to be eroded. It is vital to remember that repeating old mistakes, getting stuck on a particular issue or behavior, or being confused by the recovery process are simply parts of the process and not indications that one is stupid, inadequate or a failure. The best way to deal with gnawing feelings of guilt, shame, embarrassment, impatience or frustration is to talk about them. It also helps to get feedback from others farther along in the process or from a trusted professional who can reassure and help clarify when needed.

The deeper and more thoroughly one wishes to anchor that self-esteem, the more intensive and long-term the process of achieving it is likely to be. Accomplishment of simple exercises or telling oneself repeatedly that one is okay do not lead, in themselves, to an authentic increase in self-esteem. An in-depth understanding of oneself and one's behavior, including an acceptance of one's shortcomings as well as a recognition of one's strengths requires a detailed and complex examination of one's life.

The Illusion

Use of the illusion also will not be amenable to quick or simple resolution, given how deep and connected to core issues it is. Long-term individual and group psychotherapy will have the most benefits in uncovering the illusion and examining its detrimental affect on one's behavior, relationships and self-image. Until they feel quite safe and close to those they are working with, people will not risk exposing the existence of the illusion, so protective is it of one's most vulnerable self. For adult children of alcoholics, that does not happen quickly or easily. Yet once they can begin to look honestly and openly at the illusion, they are well on their way to making the significant changes that lead to lasting change.

Pitfalls Of Externalization

The tendency will be to externalize the problems and the solution to the problems. Long-term psychotherapy will be the best way of dealing with that externalization and, therefore, lead to the most comprehensive and permanent change. All therapy is not the same and will therefore not give the same results. Certain kinds of therapy can reinforce that tendency to externalize and ultimately prove countertherapeutic. If people turn over responsibility for recovery to the therapist and the therapist accepts that responsibility, then both collude in preventing people from assuming appropriate responsibility for their therapy and ultimately their lives. That does not mean a therapist does not have responsibilities within the therapy, but those responsibilities are about the proper conduct of the therapy and not about the person's recovery. This may be hard to distinguish. The use of examples may help.

Often, a survival technique that worked for children growing up was the suppression of feelings. Chronic suppression of feelings can lead to serious psychological and even physical consequences. Once people understand this and see a better understanding of the nature and management of feelings as one goal of the therapy, they may then think that it is the therapist's responsibility to "make them feel." This, in fact, is not true. Ultimately they will have to decide that they can trust the therapist enough to begin to express some feelings. Therapists who structure exercises to "make" people feel are only feeding into the illusion that it is their responsibility to make people change. This infantilizes people, giving them the message that they are incapable of dealing with this difficult problem. When they can see that the decision to deal with their difficulties around feelings is their choice, then they may feel less like victims and not only take the responsibility but also the credit for their progress. If they only look to the therapist to do it for them, they will never develop confidence in themselves and their own abilities.

A therapist does have responsibilities, but those responsibilities include helping persons recognize when they are feeling; making sure feelings do not get cut off as they begin to emerge; and helping people look at what those feelings are and mean and how they relate to past and current experiences. The therapist's responsibility is to help the person increase self-understanding and self-awareness, not through telling and giving advice but by continually encouraging the person to explore behavior, motivation and feelings and pointing out when reasoning seems faulty, when conclusions don't follow logically from the facts and when feelings seem inappropriately absent or intense.

The Difficulties Of Taking Help

Change does not occur in a vacuum. One must "take help" in order to change, whether it is simply reading or listening to someone else's ideas, participating in a self-help group or engaging in psychotherapy. Here again there are perils. The idea of getting help for problems, while not easy for anyone, may be particularly difficult for children of alcoholism. With little or no experience of a trustworthy, consistent caretaker it may be hard and even impossible to believe that someone else can really help. This will be elaborated further in Chapter 11, but needs to be mentioned here because it may prevent someone from even considering taking any kind of help.

"I should be able to do it myself," is a sentiment voiced frequently by children of alcoholism when it is suggested that they need to consider entering therapy or going to a self-help group. This automatic response points to the early experiences. These children learned early that they had to be self-sufficient and that to rely on the unreliable adult was often foolhardy and frequently dangerous. This outlook becomes generalized and unconsciously, rigidly applied. "Never rely on others for help" becomes the powerful, never-questioned internal message. Since change requires just that, it goes against the basic survival instinct of being independent and self-sufficient. To trust another person, to allow intimacy with another person goes against everything they learned as children about how to survive in an inconsistent and uncaring world. No matter that this is no longer the same inconsistent and uncaring world. Survival is still the primary issue and survival precludes trust, dependency and intimacy. Thus the very qualities that could lead to change, and therefore more satisfying lives, go against the deepest instincts of survival.

One solution to this very difficult problem is to start with a therapy group. Since children could often trust siblings before adults, it may be easier in the beginning to trust fellow group members than to trust the group therapists. This is perfectly all right since fellow group members will have much to offer, and a good therapy group will have leaders who will ensure that the process remains therapeutic. Individual and group therapy are often particularly effective when used concurrently to complement each other.

Because adult children of alcoholics are so self-critical, they will tend to interpret the need for therapy as just one more failure. Seeing therapy as a sign of defeat either prevents them from entering therapy or it colors the therapy so that if not repeatedly examined, it is doomed to failure. Therapy is *not* a sign of inadequacy or stupidity or weakness nor does it indicate an inability to be self-reliant. It is rather an acknowledgment that one has the capacity and desire to learn, and can change and continue to develop. Entering therapy and learning to trust others to help in that process is an indication, not of failure but of the courage to take risks and the capacity to grow.

Therapy

CHAPTER 11

Why A Chapter On Therapy?

In the last chapter I emphasized the importance of psychotherapy in doing the internal work that will ultimately lead to lasting change. While that chapter delineates the specific reasons why therapy helps and what therapy is needed for, therapy is so difficult for people growing up with alcoholism that a description of the nature of those difficulties may help both therapists and the users of therapy in making therapy more effective.

Engaging in a process that will lead to significant change is difficult for everyone. It is also painful if it entails a true examination of the self and the experiences that led one to develop the defenses now in question. Although this process is difficult and painful for everyone, it is experienced as particularly alarming by adults coming from a childhood of alcoholism who often perceive difficulty and pain as being connected to survival. As they are expected to gradually decrease the use of defenses that they have until now used to survive, people feel very much at risk and overwhelmed, as if emotional and even actual survival is at issue. It feels safer to leave treatment than to risk exposure of such a vulnerable, undefended and unprotected self. This leaves the therapy especially vulnerable to sabotage or premature termination by the people in therapy and by their unsuspecting therapists if they are unaware of the depth of the perceived peril that the people they are treating are experiencing. Hopefully a better understanding of the therapeutic enterprise will enable both participants to overcome the threats to the success of a deep and effective process.

Expectations: Conscious And Unconscious

How one anticipates and regards therapy, both consciously and unconsciously, will have significant impact on the therapy. For example, if one regards therapy as a defeat, a sign of failure or of inadequacy that one could not do it alone, then each therapy session will be experienced as a further undermining of one's already poor self-esteem. If a person is aware of that sense of defeat or inadequacy as it relates to being in therapy and can talk about it, its impact will not only be less devastating, but can be redirected toward increased self-understanding. Negative feelings about the therapy become a part of the therapeutic process. Knowledgable therapists expect this to happen and understand how to work with it. While discussing negative feelings about the therapy, or the therapist for that matter, will feel uncomfortable, it is ultimately productive. Over time and as those feelings are repeatedly examined and increasingly understood they will take on new meaning and a different perspective. It is important to remember that these are not one-time experiences, but that such feelings will recur. Reworking over time will eventually bring about lasting change. One-time revelations will not in themselves lead to integrated behavioral and relationship changes even though they may lead to increased self-understanding.

People will also bring feelings to the therapy of which they are unaware. For example, they may recognize intellectually how therapy is not a sign of inadequacy but still harbor such feelings that are not yet in conscious awareness. This, too, can be used in the therapy. While those feelings will not necessarily subside or come to conscious awareness early in the process, the intellectual understanding that something of this nature could be operating can prevent premature termination of the therapy because of the negative feelings. This is an area where therapists can be particularly helpful if they can predict and point out such issues before or as they begin to emerge. Prediction and explanation can be particularly helpful to people who may have had very little of either one in childhood. Prediction that certain feelings may arise and an explanation of why can be both reassuring and helpful to people who are afraid or ashamed of their feelings. It is important to remember, however, that even prediction and explanation can feel like criticism to people who automatically feel "wrong" or "bad" when faced with certain feelings and that this too requires frequent discussion. Equally important, remember that adult children of alcoholics often will find it very difficult to believe authority figures or to trust them enough to allow prediction and explanation to be reassuring and helpful. The awareness of this skepticism can also be used to decrease its impact on the therapeutic process.

Perceptions Of Therapy

In order to examine some of those expectations, conscious and unconscious, that influence the therapy I will return again to Mark. In the prologue Mark describes a landscape that can be seen as metaphor for how adult children of alcoholics anticipate and later experience the therapy. Mark described a land of extremes, of darkness and light, of danger and threats to one's survival juxtaposed with an environment of unconditional nurturing and comfort. This landscape represented the childhood of alcoholism. Since most of us bring to new experiences the expectation that they will in some way resemble past experiences, *despite the hope it might be otherwise,* we can anticipate that children of alcoholism will expect the therapy experience to resemble other, older experiences.

The darkness in Mark's story can be seen to represent the inaccessibility of an accurate perception of the past, memory so shadowed by denial or repression that one is unable to make sense of it or to attach meanings to it. The danger signifies feelings threatening to emerge and overwhelm. The light represents a hope for a future more satisfying. The all-nurturing couple symbolizes the wished-for, magical, omnipotent healer that is for now the therapist. And just as Mark had to traverse a landscape fraught with physical danger and discomfort to get to the warm, all-nurturing couple who took him in, so, too, people embarking on therapy anticipate as equally dangerous the emotional territory they must now traverse. This difficult and uncomfortable terrain is comprised, not of wind and rain and icy water but of equally threatening phenomena: previously denied or repressed feelings, buried memories and sealed-over pain.

Perceptions Of The Therapist

Initially, one may bring to the therapeutic situation the same kind of idealized impressions that Mark attributed to his dreamlike farm couple. The wish for an ideal, all-nurturing, all-knowing parent may be so strong that initially the therapist will be viewed that way. At first, the therapist will be expected to know all, understand all and, most importantly, to have perfect solutions for all problems. Even if these expectations are not conscious, the hope one brings to the therapy may be somewhat unrealistic and based on the ideal rather than the actual. Understanding that the ultimate solutions will come from the self, should help to modify that unrealistic expectation of the therapist.

Eventually another kind of expectation emerges. This may remain out of conscious awareness for a very long time and even if it becomes conscious is often not talked about in the therapy. However, if it is not discussed, it could render the therapy ineffective. For many people who had the kind of childhood described here, adults and particularly the authority figure that the therapist inevitably becomes, are seen as inconsistent, untrustworthy, deceptive and dangerous. Adults are not experienced as consistent, dependable sources of consolation and comfort; they are not looked to as role models for the management of the terrifying feelings that threaten to emerge if one begins to look back on and examine one's life. Adults retaliate when hurt or confronted; they disappoint when relied on; they lie when trusted. In addition, and this is particularly important to remember for its presentation in the therapy may be extremely subtle or very carefully hidden: Adults are needy, vulnerable, incapable of caring for themselves and therefore in constant need of others (most particularly their "children") to protect them from the world and from themselves.

These deeply-embedded beliefs will shape and sometimes misshape the therapy unless they can be examined and reexamined with the therapist, for they will repeatedly recur. Unrecognized and uninterpreted they can lead to premature termination of the therapy because they lead to such thoughts as: "The therapist is no good, is using me, only cares about the money, can't really understand me or is incapable of helping me." Even worse, these misperceptions can lead to an unauthentic therapy in which the person unconsciously modifies what he or she says and does to protect the therapist. This is particularly difficult because neither participant in the therapy may be aware of it. Therapy cannot be effective if this is happening and is not addressed. Because adult children of alcoholics are so good at taking care of others, therapists may never discern this subtle form of caretaking and therefore help them to bring those feelings about the therapist into the therapy.

In order to survive, children spare themselves the conscious aware-ness of many of these thoughts and feelings about their parents and later other important people in their lives. But, they live with those perceptions and let them influence their lives and the quality of their relationships. At some point they will expect the therapy to replicate the life. No matter how dissimilar the therapist is to the person's previous experiences with important adults, the expectation of the old relationship repeating itself will remain, hidden perhaps from view but affecting the therapeutic relationship nonetheless.

It may be helpful early in the therapy to make note of this possibility. In discussing their initial reactions to group therapy several people spoke of experiencing the initial sessions as very positive, warm, gratifying, comforting and validating. Rather than reassure them, this positive experience only heightened their anxiety. As one person put it, "I kept waiting for the other shoe to drop." Each then described how they expected the situation to deteriorate, to get "bad," to become in some way harmful. At the point this was being discussed, we were trying to understand the initially high dropout rate of a long-term, insight-oriented therapy group for adult children of alcoholics. The therapists believed that the rapid dropout was the result of inadequate input from the therapists in the first session and the feeling by the group that they had been abandoned by the therapists and left to care for themselves very much the way they had been in childhood. The therapists believed that this had generated so much unconscious anger in some of the group members that they left the group rather than risk facing their own anger or unleashing it on the therapists. Although this may have been part of the truth, others in the group felt that the anxiety generated by the positive experience and the expectation that it could not last were more important. Said a survivor of that initial group, "It wasn't too bad. It was too good. It made me nervous."

Denial

A major preoccupation in an alcoholic family is the denial of the most pressing aspect of that reality for the family: the parental alcoholism. Truth is not to be revealed or uncovered, but to be denied, minimized, rationalized and even obliterated when necessary. As a result, denial of important but uncomfortable aspects of reality becomes linked to survival for a child. The child carries that defense as precious burden into adulthood, to be protected at all costs. In contrast, therapy expects the adult to eventually reveal the truth, face the painful memories and uncover the unsavory experiences. Therefore, from its very inception and as its ultimate goal, therapy will be attempting to undermine the use of the adult's most valued survival technique, the denial. At the same time, it will be challenging the *parents'* denial, their distorted perceptions as they imposed them on their children. I spoke in Chapter 1, "The Illusion," of the dilemma posed for children forced to face the contradictions in what they perceive and what their parents said about what they perceived. In therapy the old solutions to that dilemma will be challenged. Once again, now adult "children" will be forced to face those same old unsettling questions: "Were my parents lying to me?" "Did I see what I thought I saw?" "Can I trust my own perceptions?" "Am I crazy?"

Confusion As Solution

As people face those old questions, we can expect them to bring with them the old solutions, the most prominent being a perceived confusion and reluctance to trust their perceptions. While the word confusion is used frequently by children of alcoholism, if one looks more carefully, one discovers that other internal events lie buried beneath the confusion. Confusion is used here to address two phenomena: first, the old, contested memories where parents contradicted what children perceived and second, the strong, negative emotions that threaten to emerge.

In the first instance one has to answer the questions once again, "Are my parents lying to me?" "Am I really seeing what I think I'm seeing?" Rather than answer these questions, it may be safer to revert to confusion. Confusion serves as retreat from taking a stand, from directly opposing the parents or challenging their integrity and from answering questions to which there are no good, no simple, no untainted answers. Confusion becomes a compromise in a situation where any answer is compromised.

In the second instance, strong feelings arise when one's perceptions are contradicted: "Daddy is just sleeping," or "Mommy is not herself today." Initial confusion will understandably be followed by helplessness and rage in a child not equipped to manage such powerful, confusing and contradictory messages. Confusion may attach to powerful feelings that have no safe outlet and whose origins were very appropriately connected with confusion. Confusion may then automatically be experienced with similar feelings, no matter what their origin, and may serve in addition to mask those feelings that find no direct or satisfactory outlet. Ambivalence may also be mistaken for confusion.

Carl provided an example of this. When he found his father passed out on the living room sofa, he thought he was dead and ran terrified to his mother, who then told him in spite of all Carl believed or perceived, that his father was merely sleeping. Carl describes painful and profound confusion at that moment. He then further describes how confusion arises in therapy for him and with what results: "When he (the therapist) asks me how I feel, I feel awful, like nothing." Next he describes how at a loss he feels when he cannot define or describe what he is feeling and how devastating this is for him. Lost in his perceived confusion and unable to identify or name feelings, he cannot respond honestly to the therapist, except by speaking of the confusion. If the therapist, perceiving the emotion behind the confusion, attempts to pursue this too soon, it will further reinforce Carl's sense of inadequacy about himself, in particular about his ability to identify, name and experience emotion. When Carl says "I feel awful, like nothing," he is connecting the inability to describe his feelings with an inability to describe himself, to not having a sense of his own identity. This may explain his powerfully negative reaction when asked about his feelings.

It is a common error that therapists make with adult children of alcoholics. Although it is important to help them become aware of and identify their feelings as they are experiencing them, to insist that they describe their feelings when they cannot, only increases the sense of inadequacy. Such insistence may also support the tendency to make something up in order to satisfy the therapist or at least to cover up a reaction they experience as a profound shortcoming. For Carl to invent an emotion at this point would compromise the integrity of the therapy and decrease his trust that the therapist can be helpful. At the same time, if the therapist misses the protective nature of the confusion and leaves it unquestioned, that will only further confuse the issue.

Silence

It is important to keep in mind that speech, while it is at the core of therapy and is usually the basic tool by which therapy proceeds, is often contaminated and double-edged. Speech, as experienced in the middle of an active addiction becomes the vehicle for denial, for lies, for deceptions and broken promises. Speech double binds, holds out false hope and promise and thrusts children into the illusion, the paradox and the irresolvable contradiction. Speech also allows children and later adults to hide, behind words and phrases or colorful images meant to deceive, distance or distract rather than to inform, clarify or bring close. Speech can be used to bore the listener with the tedium and the helplessness of a life lived as eternal victim. Tedious words and boring stories can distance the listener without the speaker ever having to acknowledge the hostility (or fear or sense of helplessness) behind the speech or the need to keep the listener at arms' length.

The thought of true self-revelation as product of speech may bring with it overwhelming anxiety. The thought of real closeness as the result of open and honest speech may produce intolerable tension. The thought of another person truly understanding may produce unbearable distress. "If someone gets close to me," one may reason, "gets to know me, gets to understand me, he will know what a phony I am, what a nothing I am. He will find out about my emptiness. He will learn about all my unacceptable feelings, my terror, my rage and my unending, insatiable neediness." Thus, speech, the vehicle of therapy, becomes a torturous trap. It evokes anxiety, fear and the threat of unleashing a pain that seems unmanageable and that could precipitate the termination of the therapy.

Because of the compromised nature of speech, the therapist would do well to attend less to the words and more to nonverbal behavior and to actions. Just as feelings and expectations about the therapy should be discussed, so too the meaning and the feelings about words and speech should be examined. And again, not just one time, but repeatedly through the course of the therapy until integrity is finally associated with words and speech.

The Caretaker Revisited

The role of caretaker may not present itself explicitly in the therapy but always must be accounted for. The role of tending to others starts early for children of alcoholism and becomes deeply woven into the fabric of their relationships, whether it be three-year-old Sally shaking a tiny but powerful finger at her mother as she tells her she must stop using drugs, or twelve-year-old Alicia assuming her mother's responsibilities by making a birthday party for a younger sister or fourteen-year-old Julie writing poetry to make her mother so proud she will stop drinking. Tending others becomes a defense against the awareness of children's own dependency needs; it becomes a way of structuring relationships and of organizing work and social lives. Inevitably, but imperceptibly, it enters the therapy.

Considering that adults who had an alcoholic parent in childhood are hypersensitive to the vulnerabilities of others, it is more than likely that they will intuitively recognize the therapist's unresolved concerns or vulnerability around certain themes. They will then instinctively "protect" the therapist by never presenting those concerns or any therapeutic dilemmas they assume the therapist cannot handle. These may be correct assumptions about the therapist's Achille's heel or projections of their disowned vulnerabilities. Angry feelings toward the therapist may never be expressed or if expressed, may quickly be disowned or taken back and turned inward. Self-blame or guilt will be used as a retreat, as defense, as protection from expressing anger or disappointment in a therapist presumed to be too fragile to tolerate such feelings. Ongoing verbalized assurances to the therapist about the helpfulness of the therapy, particularly when the therapist senses the discomfort with the therapy (adamantly disavowed or rationalized away as in "I know therapy has to be painful,") may be attempts to protect the therapist not only from the rage but also from the belief in the inadequacy of the therapist. Especially in the early stages of therapy, this may be unconscious and surrounded by layer upon layer of defense to keep it from rising to awareness. But even when it is conscious this very likely will not be expressed. The perception of a *powerful but inadequate* therapist will most likely exert a forceful influence on the therapy and ultimately render the therapy ineffective if not uncovered and gradually resolved.

Insight

Mark, in his story of running away from home, sets the scene for a perception focused always outward, toward the threatening and hostile environment and never inward and toward the self. To face always outward, to run away, to look away serves as a model for survival and is thus never to be questioned or altered. Mark, as he describes how he traversed a dangerous landscape, never looks inward, never discusses feelings or their management, never discusses the inner resources that helped carry him through that hard time, but instead describes only the wind and the rain and the oncoming train and the icy river. By what Mark chooses *not* to focus on he makes a strong statement about how a person survives: by the repression of insight and emotion. Once again we see how therapy, which encourages the recognition of emotion and the development of self-understanding, will be expecting Mark to perform in ways that his very instincts inform him will compromise his well-being and his actual survival.

Billy's descriptions of his childhood coping mechanisms further demonstrate this. Billy learned that the way to get through the scary nights when his parents fought and his mother threatened or acted out suicidal impulses, was to climb into bed and pull the covers over his head. This muffled the sounds of the arguments and threats and it also served as model for how he subsequently covered over his unmanageable feelings. Billy learned to muffle distress coming both from without and from within. By the time Billy reached therapy he had become so proficient at the muffling that he rarely "heard" his own feelings and then only when they presented themselves in the extreme.

Billy was forced finally to recognize how maladaptive his survival techniques had become by the near suicide of his wife. Again, even self-observation takes the route of starting with another's behavior. Billy chose group therapy as a way to begin to work on himself. Recognizing he needed to change and that therapy was a way to do it, he protected himself from the intensity of a one-to-one relationship with an individual therapist and entered a group where the intensity of the intimacy was diluted and softened by the presence of others like himself. It is easier at first to trust others like oneself and not to have to deal directly with the dreaded and untrustworthy authority figure of the therapist. It is probably the presence of the other group members that keeps many people in therapy during those most difficult early times. The group also enabled Billy to start the journey inward by first looking out to gain insight and to see himself through others. Group in this way works *with* the defense by allowing its members to begin to see themselves through others. One person said of the experience, "This group is like a mirror." "I see myself in you," is a frequently heard remark. This is initially more tolerable, more ego-syntonic, and paves the way for an eventual turning of the vision inward, toward the self. The group experience also begins to chip away at the critical messages to the self: "When I listen to other people's stories I feel less like I'm wrong and realize there were things I just didn't learn or learned wrong."

Introspection Versus Insight

It is important to make a distinction between introspection and insight. In many of the people discussed here the lack of insight does not necessarily imply a lack of thinking about the self. Emma, described as the mother of a young drug addict who herself felt ongoing suicidal impulses as both adolescent and adult, seemed totally unaware of her feelings or her state of mind. She insisted she was happy as she spoke of wanting to commit suicide and while tears rolled down her cheeks. But Emma was exceedingly introspective. She spoke of the importance of certain modern philosophers and how she pondered their writings and applied their philosophies to her own life. She further described how they helped her come to terms with her choice not to commit suicide.

Alicia, who avoided therapy despite her displeasure with her life and her inability to change, described an obsessive preoccupation with herself and her behavior. At first this sounded like Alicia had insight, but it became apparent that her ruminations stayed mostly on the surface and tended to focus more on others than on herself. Even when she could acknowledge her own tendencies to control in a relationship, still she spoke from the unconscious position of a victim. She looked outward not inward for the source of trouble, rather than being able to see in a deep or meaningful way her own contributions to the situations she kept experiencing.

Becky illustrated this same phenomenon of apparent but not real insight as she repeatedly examined her reactions and her interactions with significant others. She looked for patterns in relationships or in the games people played *on* her. Her focus was always on herself as victim, on the other and the games *he* played, and the patterns in which *she* became involved. Her vision was not turned truly inward; it was turned on herself but herself narcissistically, herself as others did to her or herself as helpless victim. She struggled with psychological concepts to gain some control over a life for which she did not and could not assume full responsibility. She brought this position and this perception to the therapy, unable to move beyond her rage as victim to a better understanding of what drove her. When she did not make the progress she felt she should make in therapy she also felt victimized by her therapist; she was unable to recognize that it was she who was resisting change because of her tenacious belief that her defenses and her perceptions are what enabled her to survive.

The tendency to externalize makes people vulnerable to therapies that promise quick or easy cures and to seeing self-help groups as the total solution. Self-help groups, reading and conference attendance, short-term structured groups and directive therapies promote cognitive understanding and encourage introspection without providing the opportunity to develop insight and the eventual working through of issues. These experiences will allow people to put names to behaviors that have troubled and confused them and to feelings that have disturbed and embarrassed them and this is good. But the tendency will be to stop with the naming and the identification because to go further will lead to painful insights. Unfortunately, stopping at this point will not lead to the working through of the problem and to ultimate resolution.

Adult children of alcoholics are often so relieved when they can name a feeling or attribute a reason to an unreasonable behavior that the relief can be taken for resolution. It is not resolution. Resolution means that those inappropriate feelings and behaviors will eventually be understood in a deeper way and will then have less power to control one's life. Identification and naming do not necessarily indicate a true turning inward toward a more in-depth (even though more anxiety-provoking) examination of the self. If used as ends in themselves, labeling, facile identification and intellectualizing may actually stand in the way of people reaching a better understanding of themselves and their own resources. Labels may replace the emptiness one feels when one faces the lack of identity, but labels are a shallow replacement for a real discovery of a more authentic self. This self *can* be discovered, but not through labels and simple formulas.

Dangers Of The Empathic Response And The Value Of Validation

I would like to return to Emma for a moment because she illustrates another dilemma in this therapy. When I responded empathically to Emma in our early sessions, she denied the presence of feelings and withdrew. Empathy may frequently be contraindicated in the early stages of treatment because it threatens to destroy defenses too quickly and puts people in contact with feelings they are not yet ready to face. Emma was not ready to experience the feelings she was so capable of describing and by its mirroring effect, empathy brings Emma closer to those feelings. Emma made it clear by her response that she was not ready to enter such "dangerous" territory. This is very different from therapy in which people not from this kind of background experience empathy as comforting and the therapist who is able to be empathic as someone who is worthy of trust and who provides an atmosphere in which it is both safe and satisfying to experience feelings. However, children of alcoholics experience feelings as trauma and those who evoke emotion as cruel and critical. And so the empathy, that would be a therapeutic response for most people, becomes nontherapeutic and even threatening for children of alcoholism.

The therapist must be able to maintain a delicate balance, for while empathy is not helpful at first, it is extremely important to be able to validate what adult children of alcoholism say. The response in childhood was repudiation or denial. Validation, clarification and affirmation become corrective experiences, a therapeutic response, which may then allow them to continue to explore the experience rather than to shut down (as Emma did) in response to empathy. When people describe painful experiences, it may sometimes appear that they are looking for the relief one might expect to get from expression of feeling. In fact, because expression of feeling is more often traumatic than relieving, what they may be looking for is validation or an acknowledgment that this could or did happen. This is a very different experience than they had with parents whose perceptions often conflicted with their own. Affirmation and validation help challenge the early experience of the parents' denial, while clarification helps to diminish the confusion that was often the child's response to the denial. Validation, affirmation and clarification become as important and necessary an experience for children of alcoholism as does ventilation for other users of therapy. Clarification, affirmation and particularly validation become the corrective emotional experience at this stage in the treatment.

Memory As Enemy Or Ally

Group therapy provides a particularly effective way to work with the frequent absence or distortion of memory as described in Chapter 6, "Memory Compromised." Very often, because the stories are so strikingly similar, one group member's tale will suddenly jog or clarify the memory of another who experienced a similar incident. Once verbalized by someone else and subject to the gentle examination that groups can be so wonderful at providing, the memory seems less threatening and therefore more able to be retrieved and addressed. This is true for the memory of incidents as well as emotions.

Billy had been in a group for relatives of the chemically dependent for over a year. A few months after entering the group he had described watching his mother make drunken suicide threats. This initial presentation was delivered flatly, without any feelings evident as he talked. He did not bring it up again. Many months later he listened to another member of his group describe how traumatized she had felt when her parents began to fight with and threaten each other. Suddenly I noticed that Billy had lost the color in his face. While, most typically for Billy, he showed no expression, his sudden paling suggested something internal was occurring. When I asked him what was happening, he said that he was not sure, but as this woman talked he suddenly felt his stomach tighten and grow tense. When encouraged to elaborate, he then remembered the old scene with his mother. This time (and for the first time) he connected a visceral reaction to the old trauma. This was Billy's first *affective* memory of this traumatic incident. Significantly it did not occur when he first brought it to the group, but later, as he heard someone else describing her own memory and the feelings connected to it. With his own feelings unavailable to him, Billy was able to use someone else's feeling to trigger his own.

In just the same way, group therapy can cut through the denial that has compromised the memory. Rick illustrated this in Chapter 6, "Memory Compromised." Never knowing what to make of his drug-addicted mother's behavior because he had never defined it as addicted, he was astounded to hear other people describe their parents. When program staff had suggested to Rick that his mother's behavior sounded as if she were addicted, he laughed, scoffed and dismissed the suggestion. But when he heard fellow group members describe incidents that paralleled incidents from his childhood, the denial dissolved and he was left with a very different sense of this very familiar memory.

The redefining of memory in a group can also serve as validation, as one way to begin to attack the confusion, self-doubt and self-deprecation that come from not having one's early perceptions validated. Remember Carl's terror when he saw his father passed out after a night of heavy drinking. Remember Carl's confusion when his mother insisted his father was only sleeping. Remember Carl's persistent confusion as an adult and how this compromised a firm sense of his identity. The relief Carl feels when other members of his therapy group affirm the validity of both his perceptions and his confusion can lead to the beginning of a more reasoned and reasonable confidence in his own perceptions.

Self-Esteem And The Illusion

In a home where parents are focused more on an active addiction than on the upbringing of the children, the self-esteem of the children is jeopardized. Children frequently feel valued, not for themselves, but only in relation to the addiction or to the narcissistic needs of the parents. In order to insure their own survival, children learn to deny or minimize their own needs and instead focus on satisfying the parents' needs so that the parents remain at least minimally available to the children.

Children will not learn to value themselves if they have not first been valued by their parents. Lack of validation by the parents of the child's perceptions and an absence of empathy regarding the emotional experiences further erodes the child's self-esteem. Both the sober and the alcoholic parent may be critical of the child. This is not because of the child's innate shortcomings but because the child becomes the recipient of the parents' projected feelings about themselves and their failure to control the addiction. Rather than acknowledge to themselves their feelings of inadequacy and failure, the parents attribute them to the children. The parents become either hypercritical or overly demanding of perfectionism regarding the children's achievements. Some blatantly blame the children for their own drinking. The children believe the parents' projections which ravages their self-esteem. As protection against this devastatingly battered sense of self, children wrap themselves in an illusion of competence and adequacy. They become, as described earlier, family heroes and caretakers, successful overachievers or black sheep; all are attempts to project a false image to others and often to the self so that they need not face the overwhelming sense of emptiness and worthlessness that the illusion masks.

They come into therapy tightly wrapped in this illusion. It serves as defense, as resistance, but particularly as protection against the anticipated devastating revelations about themselves that they feel neither they *nor* their therapists can accept or tolerate. When asked by his therapist how he is feeling, Carl is unable to respond the way he presumes his therapist expects. He feels inadequate and "like nothing." He expects his therapist to see him as inadequate because this is the way he sees himself. He further expects the therapist to be intolerant of that inadequacy, for, again, he is so intolerant of himself.

Again the paradox prevails. Therapists purposely ask hard questions. Pointed, challenging questions can help people to look more carefully at themselves, to question their own automatic and unconscious responses and to reevaluate driven, unthinking and self-defeating behavior. Difficult questions can lead to more accurate, honest self-observation. While this may be initially disquieting and uncomfortable, such honest self-appraisal in turn leads to increased self-understanding and ultimately self-acceptance. For children of alcoholism the process gets turned around and questions that should ultimately lead toward better self-esteem instead lead to increasing the sense of the self as inadequate. Questions that cannot be easily answered should provide some discomfort, but also challenge, curiosity and an impetus to explore further. For children of alcoholism such questions lead instead to feeling criticized and unintelligent or "like nothing." The impetus becomes to cover up the real self and to distance even further from self-acceptance. Rather than learning more and accepting oneself in all one's complexity, with strengths and with shortcomings, the tendency is to wrap the illusion even tighter around oneself, to hide from both the therapist and the self.

Typical in this respect, Carl has fears that go beyond the sense of inadequacy. Usually hiding behind illusion and silence, Carl has become more open and trusting in a therapy group for adult children of alcoholics, with others who seem to share so many of his characteristics and concerns. He has just finished describing the contrasts between the drab and dreary life at home and the glamorous, almost dream-like life on the family yacht. He voices his fear: "No wonder I'm so unrealistic," he remarks. "I spend a lot of my time living in a fantasy world. I get so involved in my fantasies that I start acting like they're real. I'll imagine that I'm rich and powerful and then I'll start acting arrogant." He shakes his head. "I'm nothing and I act arrogant." He pauses. When he looks up there is fear and doubt in his eyes as he says, "I feel like I'm crazy."

No one has been there to validate or reassure him. No one has helped him to sort out his confusion or his difficulty reconciling the many contradictions in his life. The result is not only confusion but questions as to his very sanity and as to whether or not at his core he is "all right." His defense against such fears is to gather further the illusion around him, to look good and to act "arrogant" so as not to experience the inadequacy. But this solution only reinforces the sense of inadequacy for it forces him to play a part. If he is then accepted he will believe it is not for himself but for the part he plays. When his therapist asked him how he felt, Carl did not experience this as someone genuinely interested in him and in helping him, but rather focused on his inability to respond properly, and thus he felt even more inadequate. Until he can grapple with these fears *and the need to mask them* he will in therapy as in life, continue to erode his self-esteem rather than to build it.

He will force himself in the therapy as he has in other situations into no-win positions. Rather than respond honestly to the therapist's interest in his feelings he will either say something that sounds appropriate (he's become proficient at second-guessing what others want him to say) or he might respond by silence. In either case the result is destructive to his self image. If he gives the therapist what he thinks the therapist wants to hear (a phenomenon I believe occurs frequently in the treatment of children of alcoholics), then he feels phony. He convinces himself repeatedly that the therapist could never respect him if the therapist *really* knew him. If he responds with silence or even with an honest "I don't know," he reinforces his sense of being inadequate. Carl, so long living with irreconcilable dilemmas, now also creates them. To be authentic, to be honest to himself and to his therapist, will evoke in him a deep sense of inadequacy. To cover up those feelings, to maintain the illusion, protects him from those feelings but gives him instead the sense of being false, being unreal, of even being crazy.

I think again of ten-year-old Jamie alternately stacking his cookies as if they were toy building blocks and then elucidating family dynamics as if he were a wise old man looking back over his life. I remember the hint of fear in his eyes as he described driving with his mother when she was drunk. I also remember how quickly he moved to defend her and possibly ward me off when I sympathized with his predicament. Is Jamie at age ten already building an illusion around himself, excluding me as he piles up his strengths as a barrier, much like he stacks his cookies? Is he hoping he will look so good and sound so good that no one will look behind the barricade and see his fears, his unacceptable feelings and his voracious neediness? Even at age ten Jamie was good at keeping me away, keeping me at a safe distance, not allowing me to see more than he decided I should see.

However Jamie had another potential solution available to him, as he showed me: Jamie reached out; Jamie talked to me. Talking, still instinctive for Jamie at age ten, is a route out of the dilemma and away from the illusion. As he gets older and if there is no therapeutic intervention that instinct to talk will shut down. The ambivalence he now demonstrates around talking will have resolved and he will instead surround himself with silence. Older "Jamies" will have to make a conscious effort to break the silence and rediscover the instinct to reach out to another human being, to use speech to cut through the illusion to discover the self.

Finally, I return to Alex, the paraplegic young alcoholic with the violent father who at age seven would watch the clock and call the police if the lateness of the hour convinced him that his father would be so drunk when he arrived that he might do violence to Alex's mother. Alex was described as an example of someone who acted out his feelings rather than risk expressing them. He also spoke of how he wished his plane would crash when he finally realized that his role as caretaker for his mother and sisters was coming to an end. Alex's defenses were so extreme and untouchable that they had brought him repeatedly to the brink of death. Even after his near-fatal car accident they remained untouched and unquestioned. He did not enter treatment because he recognized the need for help; he came in because his continued flirtation with death and disaster had so terrified his parents that they were finally able to break through their own denial and insist he enter a hospital.

When Alex recounted his feelings of wanting the plane to crash when he realized he could no longer take comfort or retreat in his old coping mechanisms he reminds us that this issue is not settled for him. Recovery brings its own perils, as ominous, as potentially threatening as remaining untreated. He warns that the lowering of defenses too rapidly and the stripping of the old adaptations without replacement by healthier ones may also prove deadly. At this stage in Alex's life, death, like the silence earlier, seems to hover around him, whether it is in the maintenance of his defenses or in their elimination.

The Breaking Of The Silence

While Alex emphasizes the high risks involved in treatment, he also exemplifies the benefits. Remember that Alex's most trusted defense was his denial. He denied not only his alcoholism but through his daredevil behavior and his caretaking, he also denied all awareness of unacceptable feelings. As a child, he learned that silence helped to maintain the denial. Were little Alex to ask his mother what had happened the morning after a violent scene, she might dissolve into tears. That would make it worse. Then Alex would be hurting her too. Better, if she seems to be managing, just to let it alone. Better if they both pretend everything is all right. Maybe even get to believe it. Or start to wonder what is real and what isn't. On the other hand, were Alex to ask his father what had happened, he would risk the full extent of his father's rage being turned on him. That would be unwise. Thus, Alex learned at an early age that the issue of his father's drinking was never to be discussed. Yet his father's drinking was the most important thing in Alex's life. It controlled everything else that happened in the family and directly affected the amount and quality of the attention spent on Alex and his needs. Alex thus learned not to talk about the most important thing in his life. He paid a price for this kind of survival that he pays for still. Not talking isolates him. It prevents him from getting healthy feedback from others and from correcting the distorted perceptions and assumptions he makes. It reinforces the feeling that he is different, set apart from others by the severity of his home life. It entrenches the guilt that somehow the terrible things that happen in his family are his fault.

As a result, a silence gradually surrounds Alex. This silence grows out of ear-shattering noises: crashing of objects in the middle of the night, breaking of windows, loud and harsh arguing voices, thunderous threats, shrill screams and, perhaps, loudest of all for young Alex, quiet sobbing. To contain the noise, to control it and to keep it from overwhelming him, he surrounds it with silence. The silence seems to work for him, gets him through the crazy times, the noisy times. But, unbeknownst to Alex, it also cripples him, stunts his growth and impoverishes him. The silence protects him but it also buries him.

For Alex, the denial and the accompanying silence, while enabling him to survive his childhood, were preventing him from surviving his alcoholism. The prohibitions to speak or to face his feelings were so powerful that even a crippling, near-fatal accident could not loosen them and may even have reinforced them. When Alex finally entered inpatient treatment for his alcoholism, the prohibition followed him. The more he was encouraged to speak in individual and group settings, the more rigid his defenses became. And the more silent he became. Until he entered a therapy group for adult children of alcoholics.

Alex began the group with two other men who had violent fathers. Neither of the other two had experienced the extreme consequences of their own alcoholism that Alex had. Both held down good jobs. Neither had had a serious accident or illness brought about by the alcoholism. Both were married. Both were significantly older than Alex. All three had been in the hospital program at least two weeks, but had never before spoken except superficially to each other. Gradually, quietly, as the group progressed, the barriers that until then had so rigidly separated these three men began to disappear. As Alex listened to twenty-nine year old Billy describe his father, his eyes widened in amazement and recognition, listening to someone describing experiences he had had but had never shared with anyone.

Said Billy, "My father would punch me while I slept. He'd beat up my mother. I would lie awake nights waiting for him to come home, listening for his footsteps. I could tell by the way he walked if he was drunk or sober. As I lay in bed, my heart would pound so hard I thought it would wake the entire house!" He laughed in embarrassment and tapped his chest, "It's pounding just thinking about it."

With eyes riveted on Bill, Alex began to talk as if continuing Bill's story, as if the stories were one and the same. "I used to watch the clock," said Alex. "I could tell by how late it got whether he'd come home drunk or not." Interrupted Bob, thirty-three and the third man to start the group that day, "Yes, and if he did, watch out!" Alex looked at him, startled, then smiled in agreement. Bob continued, "The furniture would go flying out the window. And he'd beat up on my mother." Alex interrupted, "When that started I'd call the police. Sometimes, if it was late enough, I'd know how drunk he'd probably be and I'd call the police even before he got home to warn them that there might be trouble. So they'd be ready, you know." The others knew. They shook their heads in recognition.

Suddenly the silence was broken. The commonality of the experiences loosened the defenses. It was done very quietly. Each man spoke almost in a whisper. Memory, usually repressed or suppressed, softly cried out. The stories, so similar, blended one into the other. The sense of being different dissipated for the moment. Vision, usually so intently turned outward, now turned in, toward the self. All three men, brawny, usually gruff and inarticulate, were suddenly shy, tentative and yet fluent as the past poured out. The remembered experiences were violent, brutal. But the atmosphere in the room was gentle, even tender.

When I asked, Alex said he was seven or eight when he began calling the police. "I had to. I was the oldest. I had three younger sisters to protect." Bob understood. He remembered making trouble at the dinner table to draw his father's wrath off his mother and onto himself. Bill laughed at that. "I used to spill the milk," he said, shaking his head. "I spilled more milk!" When asked if they weren't afraid of repercussions, neither could respond. Bob added that had he begun to whimper or cry, his father would have become even angrier. And his mother, already at her limits, might have become more distraught to see her young son in tears. He couldn't do that to her. Bill and Alex nodded in agreement.

When asked, none of them could remember much in the way of feelings being connected to these events. Each had concentrated on taking care of the rest of their family as the way to survive these traumas. None of them expressed emotion, then or now. Instead, they took action, took care of someone else as the only way available at the time to take care of themselves. When they were encouraged to try to think about feelings that might have been attached to these events, they all quickly moved to wondering out loud how a man could do such a thing, how a man could ever let himself beat up a woman. Bill's eyes filled and softly he said, "I started to do the same thing. I got drunk and I hit my wife. That's why I'm here. I never want to be like him." Alex shook his head and looked at Bill. His eyes reflected pain and confusion. "I can't understand that," he whispered. "Whenever I touch a girl, I'm very careful at first. I'm always afraid she'll break."

These men, tortured products of violence, bound by repression and silence, isolated from others by a childhood of alcoholism, are here brought together by that childhood and find comfort in being with each other. While their words never said this, their behavior did. Each one's attention was riveted to the others as they spoke. Each sat in breathless silence as he heard his story verbalized by someone else. They viewed each other in rapt concentration. Slight nods of the head and half-smiles belied the intensity of their fascination with each other. It was as if they were taking each other in, as if devouring the commonality of the experiences. The shared experience of the violence produced compassion and understanding for each other. The silence and isolation, brought on by the parental alcoholism, were broken by the commonality of the parental alcoholism. In this group, where truth was neither denied nor invalidated, speech achieved integrity. Trust became a possibility.

The therapeutic aspect is not, as a therapist might expect, the ventilation of feelings nor the expression of long-repressed emotions, for that would still be too traumatic. What was therapeutic for these three men was the validation, the validation that came from hearing their own experiences described by someone else. The nods, the smiles, the finishing of each others' sentences, this validates. Experiencing each other in this way affirms; it is healing; it is therapeutic. What is also therapeutic is the breaking of the life-long isolation and the challenge to the notion that one is different (and worse) from other people. Although a brief experience such as this will not eliminate those feelings permanently, to have had the experience of being part of something, of belonging and not feeling different can now become a possibility because it has already been experienced.

This experience is not cure. It is the model for a beginning. Alex had further difficulties and had to be rehospitalized for his alcoholism. But this need not be a sign of failure or an indication that there is no hope for Alex. This is simply a sign of the depth of the defenses that Alex had to use as a child to survive and the tenaciousness of their influence in the present. The fact that this group could "open up my world, a little bit," as Alex described it, is tribute to both the healing powers of that shared experience and also to Alex's ability to let these other men touch him. This experience laid vital groundwork for the next time Alex entered treatment. The second time, Alex himself recognized his need for help and his desire to be helped; this never would have occurred to him previously.

Alex's struggles emphasize that the solutions are neither quick nor easy, but that they exist. For some, whose background and adaptations were not as severe, therapy becomes an enriching, liberating experience, a chance to acquire real understanding, and a means to assume control and responsibility for one's life. For Alex, treatment may have saved his life.

CHAPTER 12

Beyond
Survival

I have frequently illustrated in these chapters how growing up in an alcoholic family calls for the development of impressive skills on the part of children. I have also elaborated on how these survival skills often become liabilities when applied to healthier, non-alcoholic situations. It is important to remember that the negative outcomes described in these pages are the response to the exigencies of an unfavorable childhood and not, as children of alcoholism will be too quick to assume, a consequence of innate inadequacy.

My concern is that children of alcoholism, already so self-critical, might be tempted to use the material in this book to further criticize themselves, to further diminish their self-esteem and to feel hopeless about the possibility of change. My intention is just the opposite. There can be no denying that there are significant problems, often deeply-rooted problems, that because they are so old and go so deep have become entrenched, even cherished. But it must be remembered that these problems were initially solutions, and successful solutions at that, for they enabled children to survive. Paradoxically, the intransigence of the problems also points to the strength that people have within themselves to overcome those problems. For accompanying each negative consequence of a childhood of alcoholism, there is a corresponding strength that serves as potential to rework the liabilities so that they become assets instead. The child's ability to problem solve, to persevere in the face of real difficulty and even danger, to endure despite overwhelming hardship, to tolerate the paradox and the impossible dilemma, can all be used now by the adult desiring to create a future better than the past and not indiscriminately determined by the past.

In order to do this, it is crucial to maintain a balanced perspective. Remember Mark, in his description of running away from home, described a landscape of extremes — all danger and darkness as he ran, all pleasantness and light with the farm couple. To only see the future or the past in terms of black and white, in terms of extremes, will itself be dangerous, will sabotage realistic possibilities for growth and change. It is necessary to keep both one's strengths and shortcomings in perspective. It is equally important to be *aware* of both one's strengths and shortcomings because all must be considered. People cannot come to a realistic appreciation of themselves unless they are willing to face themselves and their actions, good and bad, to forgive themselves their weaknesses and shortcomings, to take responsibility for their wrong doing, to recognize their strengths and abilities and to accept the whole continuum that is themselves.

The illusion, that deceptive presentation of the self, which operates both externally and internally for children of alcoholism, can easily prevent genuine self-acceptance. The tendency will be to protect themselves and others by using the illusion to conceal. This prevents an authentic acceptance of the self for the illusion is not real. It is based instead on what they think others want or expect or value. It has little to do with what the individual really is. Only gradual and persistent facing the self and getting to know the self better and better will eventuate in authentic self-acceptance.

Honest self-examination will also be impeded by the existing preconceptions and unchallenged value judgments such as — "I'm inadequate. I'm incompetent. I'm worthless. I'm bad. I can control everything and everyone around me if I just try hard enough and keep at it long enough. I can take care of everyone around me and meet all of their needs if I just try hard enough and keep at it long enough." Those ongoing messages to the self, which may be conscious or unconscious, will continue to result in compulsive, frequently irresponsible, self-destructive behavior unless challenged persistently over time as they reappear in different forms and faces.

I do not believe this can be done alone. It takes outside, objective and informed feedback to challenge those self-sabotaging messages. It requires outside input to help redefine and reappraise and put in a reasonable and realistic context the self-defeating perceptions and assumptions that so often drive a person's life. Maintaining a balanced perspective, putting things in a realistic context, seeing all sides of an issue — these are the abilities most children of alcoholism were not helped to develop. These are the skills that must now be learned in order to lead a life that will be balanced, rich and satisfying. Taking help from others in this endeavor also goes against the childhood training but is the only way to overcome the childhood maladaptations.

Losses And Death

Losses and death are themes that run throughout this book as they run throughout the lives of children of alcoholism. Even those who have not suffered the actual loss of a parent to death or divorce, have experienced, to some extent or another, the loss of the parents to the alcoholism. If children also have to take on many of the parents' responsibilities, then the children have also lost their childhood to the alcoholism.

Unmourned losses lead to depression. How often do people organized around the chaos of alcoholism have the opportunity to work through their feelings, to celebrate their joys and triumphs or to mourn their losses and deaths? For those who do not have the opportunity, depression may be a despised but constant companion; it may be a feared but frequent visitor; it may be an unrecognized but influential and ongoing presence. That depression persists until a person is able to face the unmourned losses that brought it on. Children of alcoholism, so good at tolerating crisis, chaos, hardship and misery will live with the chronic, erosive effects of depression, rather than face their losses, their fear, their rage and their emptiness. And yet it is only when they face those feelings, examine them over and over again, that they can ultimately move away from them and the malignant influence they exert on their lives.

To adult children of alcoholics facing feelings seems life-threatening. It only seems that way. It is not. The strength and tenacity used for getting through all the crises, all the problems of others, all the seemingly no-win situations, that strength and tenacity can be used to face the self and experience the feelings buried within. If one does, one inevitably finds that one is not nearly as bad or as good as one had imagined, that one's feelings are not as destructive as one had thought, that one's needs are not as unmeetable as one had feared, that one's emptiness is not as devastating as one had expected and that one's isolation need not be as impenetrable as one anticipated.

The theme of death and losses, which winds in and out of the lives of children of alcoholism, can be faced and put in its proper perspective. The ongoing, chronic toll those losses take and the influence they exert on one's mood and functioning, can be addressed and modified so that they become less important, and a less controlling part of one's being. Coping with death and loss can mature a person, can strengthen a person, can add depth and meaning to one's outlook. That can only happen if one faces the losses, consciously and emotionally experiences them and then allows the experience to become a part of one's understanding and appreciation of oneself.

The children of alcoholics movement has done an invaluable service to people growing up with an alcoholic parent. It has raised the nation's awareness of the toll taken on children by a parent's alcoholism. Calling attention to the fact of the phenomena has reduced some of the stigma, mystery and misunderstanding that has for so long surrounded it. It has helped to alleviate the shame and guilt that people have carried with them since childhood. It has lessened that almost impenetrable sense of isolation that accompanies them throughout the childhood and into the adulthood. This movement has given a name and a reason to a pain that has until now gone without name and without identifiable reason. This is healing. However, here, as everywhere, there can be pitfalls if one goes too far, if one loses perspective.

Awareness of being the child of an alcoholic will help to identify some of the problems that one experiences in living and in relationships. However, being the child of an alcoholic is not an identity. It is not even "**The Problem.**" It points to the possibility for a series of problems and to the possible causes for those problems, but it does not, it cannot, define those problems in a universal way for everybody. That would diminish the very nature of the problem for each person is a unique individual, with a unique history and a unique set of problems. To stop at defining oneself exclusively as the child of an alcoholic limits the self, isolates once again, cuts oneself off from one's commonality with all people, with all human suffering and all human satisfaction.

To stop with defining oneself as the child of an alcoholic limits one's self-definition. This limitation is an old problem, similar to how one saw oneself and organized one's life in relation to the alcoholism in the family. For true recovery one must reorganize beyond the alcoholism. That means ultimately being able to move beyond one's definition of oneself as the child of an alcoholic to defining the self simply as woman or man or child. To be sure, this definition includes being a man or a woman or a child who has been through a particular set of circumstances which has resulted in the development of characteristics in common with others who have been through similar circumstances. Still, in the end, one is just a man or a woman or a child.

True recovery means thinking in both more detailed and more universal ways than the framework of being defined exclusively as the child of an alcoholic will permit. One must *start* with that concept but one must not *end* with it. One must start by seeing one's commonality with other children who experienced parental alcoholism but then move beyond these generalities.

One must closely scrutinize one's own experiences and reactions without having to put them in a particular framework or vocabulary to understand them. One must face the specifics of one's own experience and one's own feelings and even one's own emptiness. One must face all that directly, not through the use of preconceived ideas about it and not through a structure or conceptualization that will categorize or constrict the experience by generalizing it or too narrowly defining it. To do this one must be ready to face the fear and anxiety of entering uncharted territory, of facing the unknown that is the self. When one does this, one finds eventually that one is facing one's own humanity, that one has moved from the particular to the universal, to one's commonality, not only with other adult children of alcoholics but with all people. For that is where one's ultimate identity must lie: with the very particulars of one's own existence and with the universality of one's humanity.

Bibliography

Ackerman, R. J. **Children of Alcoholics: A Bibliography and Resource Guide.** Pompano Beach, FL: Health Communications, 1987.

Balis, S. A. 1986. "Illusion and Reality: Issues in the Treatment of Adult Children of Alcoholics." *Alcoholism Treatment Quarterly* 3, no. 4:67-91.

Black, C. **It Will Never Happen to Me.** Denver, CO: Medical Administration, 1982.

Black, C., Bucky S., and Wilder-Padilla, S. 1986. "The Interpersonal and Emotional Consequences of Being an Adult Child of an Alcoholic." *International Journal of the Addictions* 21, no. 2:213-231.

Bowen, Murray. "Toward the Differentiation of a Self in One's Own Family." In Framo, J. (ed.). **Family Interaction.** New York: Springer, 1971.

Cermak, T. L., and Brown, S. 1982. "Interactional Group Therapy with the Adult Children of Alcoholics." *International Journal of Group Psychotherapy* 32, no. 3:375-389.

Cermak, T. L., and Rosenfeld, A. 1987. "Therapeutic Considerations with Adult Children of Alcoholics." *Advances in Alcohol and Substance Abuse* 6, no. 4:17-31.

Dewald, P. A. **Psychotherapy: A Dynamic Approach.** New York: Basic Books, 1964.

Erikson, E. H. **Childhood and Society.** New York: W. W. Norton, 1950, 1963.

Ewing, J., and Fox, R. "Family Therapy of Alcoholism." In Masserman, J. (ed.). **Handbook of Psychiatric Therapies.** New York: Science House, 1966.

Fewell, C. H., and Bissell, L. 1978. "The Alcoholic Denial Syndrome: An Alcohol-Focused Approach." *Social Casework* January: 6-13.

Frankl, V. E. **Man's Search for Meaning.** Boston: Beacon Press, 1959.

Freud, A. **The Ego and the Mechanisms of Defense.** 2nd ed. New York: International Universities Press, 1936, 1966.

Greenson, R. R. 1949. "The Psychology of Apathy." *Psychoanalytic Quarterly* 18:270-302.

Haley, J. (ed.). **Changing Families.** New York: Grune & Stratton, 1971.

Hawley, N. P., and Brown, E. L. 1981. "The Use of Group Treatment with Children of Alcoholics." *Social Casework* 62, no. 1:40-46.

Hollis, F. **Casework: A Psychosocial Therapy.** New York: Random House, 1964.

Howard, D., and Howard, N. **A Family Approach to Problem Drinking.** Columbia: Family Training Center, 1976.

Jackson, J. "Alcoholism and the Family." In Pittman, D., and Snyder, C. (eds.). **Society, Culture, and Drinking Patterns.** New York: John Wiley & Sons, 1962.

Kaufman, E., and Kaufman, P. N. **Family Therapy of Drug and Alcohol Abuse.** New York: Garner Press, 1979.

Kritsberg, W. **Chronic Shock and Adult Children of Alcoholics.** Pompano Beach, FL: Health Communications, 1985.

Krystal, H. 1974. "The Genetic Development of Affects and Affect Regression." *Annual Psychoanalysis* 2:98-126.

——————— 1978. "Self Representation and the Capacity for Self Care." *Annual Psychoanalysis* 6:209-247.

——————— 1978. "Trauma and Affects." *Psychoanalytic Study of the Child* 33:81-116.

——————— 1981. "The Aging Survivor of the Holocaust: Integration and Self-Healing in Posttraumatic States." *Journal Geriatric Psychiatry* 14, no. 1:165-209.

Lewis, D., and Williams, C. (eds.). **Providing Care for Children of Alcoholics: Clinical and Research Perspective.** Pompano Beach, FL: Health Communications, 1986.

Lister, E. D. 1982. "Forced Silence: A Neglected Dimension of Trauma." *Am. J. Psychiatry* 139, no. 7:872-876.

Mahler, M. S., Pine, F., and Bergman, A. **The Psychological Birth of the Human Infant.** New York: Basic Books, 1975.

McGoldrick, M., and Pearce, J. K. 1981. "Family Therapy with Irish Americans." *Family Process* 20:223-241.

Middelton-Moz, J., and Dwinell, L. **After the Tears.** Pompano Beach, FL: Health Communications, 1986.

Miller, A. **The Drama of the Gifted Child.** New York: Basic Books, 1981.

Russell, M., Henderson, C., and Blume, S. **Children of Alcoholics: A Review of the Literature.** New York: Children of Alcoholics Foundation, 1985.

Sacks, O. **The Man Who Mistook His Wife for a Hat and Other Clinical Tales.** New York: Summit Books, 1987.

Steinglass, P. 1976. "Experimenting with Family Treatment Approaches to Alcoholism, 1950-1975: A Review." *Family Process* **15**:97-123.

Steinglass P., Weiner, S., and Mendelson, J. 1971. "Interactional Issues as Determinants of Alcoholism." *Amer. J. Psychiatry* **128**, no. 3:275-279.

Steinglass, P. et al. **The Alcoholic Family.** New York: Basic Books, 1987.

Typpo, M. H., and Hastings, J. M. **An Elephant in the Living Room.** Minneapolis: CompCare Publications, 1984.

van der Kolk, B. **Psychological Trauma.** Washington, DC: American Psychiatric Press, 1987.

Wegscheider, S. **Another Chance: Hope and Health for the Alcoholic Family.** Palo Alto: Science and Behavior Books, 1981.

Wheelis, A. **How People Change.** New York: Harper & Row, 1973.

Winnicott, D. "Ego Distortion in Terms of True and False Self." in **The Maturational Processes and the Facilitating Environment.** New York: International Universities Press, 1960, 1965.

_____ "Ego Integration in Child Development." In **The Maturational Processes and the Facilitating Environment.** New York: International Universities Press, 1961, 1965.

_____ "Communicating and Not Communicating Leading to a Study of Certain Opposites." In **The Maturational Processes and the Facilitating Environment.** New York: International Universities Press, 1963, 1965.

Wishnie, H. "The Psychotherapy of Character." **New England Educational Institute Symposium.** Eastham, MA, July 15-19, 1985.

Woititz, J. **Adult Children of Alcoholics.** Pompano Beach, FL: Health Communications, 1983.

Wolin, S. J., Bennett, L. A., Noonan, D. L., and Teitelbaum, M. A. 1980. "Disrupted Family Rituals: A Factor in the Intergenerational Transmission of Alcoholism." *Journal of Studies on Alcohol* **41**:199-214.